CARLOS'

CARLOS'
Contemporary French Cuisine

Debbie and Carlos Nieto
with Arlene Michlin Bronstein and Ken Bookman
photography by Eric Futran

Gibbs Smith, Publisher
Salt Lake City

First Edition
09 08 07 06 05   5 4 3 2 1

Published by
Gibbs Smith, Publisher
P.O. Box 667
Layton, Utah 84041

1.800.748.5439 orders
www.gibbs-smith.com

Designed by Deibra McQuiston
Printed and bound in Hong Kong
Photography: eric@chefshots.com, www.chefshots.com

Library of Congress Cataloging-in-Publication Data

Nieto, Debbie.
  Carlos' : contemporary French cuisine / Debbie and Carlos Nieto ; with
Arlene Michlin Bronstein and Ken Bookman; photography by Eric Futran. — 1st ed.
      p. cm.
Includes index.
ISBN 1-58685-512-3
1. Cookery, French. 2. Carlos' (Restaurant) I. Nieto, Carlos, 1947 Nov.4-
II. Carlos' (Restaurant) III. Title.
TX719.N45 2005
641.5944 — dc22

2005010959

TO OUR EXTENDED FAMILIES —
IN THE UNITED STATES AND MEXICO

C O N T E N T S

ACKNOWLEDGMENTS   **8**

INTRODUCTION   **12**

INGREDIENTS & EQUIPMENT **18**

GARNISHES   **22**

AMUSE-BOUCHE   **24**

APPETIZERS   **50**

SOUPS AND SALADS   **72**

ENTRÉES   **92**

CARLOS' SPECIALS   **136**

STAFF MEALS   **150**

SIDE DISHES   **162**

DESSERTS   **172**

DRESSINGS AND OILS   **206**

BASICS   **216**

INDEX   **230**

ACKNOWLEDGMENTS

We would like to thank so many people in our business. One is the late Jimmy Rohr, our mentor. Others are Charlie Trotter, for his help and suggestions in putting together this project; Doris and Jean Banchet, the most instrumental people in starting fine dining in Chicago; Rick Tramonto and Gale Gand, who came to our rescue and literally saved our professional lives; Marshall and Jamee Field, who get our special thanks for being great partners; Norman Van Aken, Gordon Sinclair, Jean Joho, Lucette and Lucien Verge, Alan Tutzer, Didier and Jamie Durand, Michael Foley, Alan Sternweiler, Mark Baker, Jacky Pluton, Gabriel Viti, Roland Liccioni, John Hogan, Bob Burcenski, and Tom Alves, all of whom have elevated Chicago's fine-dining scene.

We also want to thank Richard and Martha Melman, a couple whose success in the restaurant business is legendary. Richard has always been willing to share his knowledge and has generously given us heartfelt advice. And special thanks to Pedro Martinez, Nabor Vasquez, and Edwardo Galvan, whose indispensable work at Café Central is very much appreciated.

Carlos' staff was the source for some amazing help. Ramiro Velasquez, our award-winning head chef, has been working with us since we began this project. His culinary talent and creativity were invaluable in writing the recipes for this book. Ron Stoddard, our sous chef and, in the summer, the head chef at our sister operation in the Freehling Room at Ravinia Festival, helped create many of these recipes. Eddie Mendoza, an incredible chef, has been so instrumental in every facet of this book. From executing recipes to reading and revising them, Eddie has exhibited more patience than any saint could possibly possess. And our well-respected wine expert and Freehling Room manager, Marcello Cancelli, has paired almost all of our recipes with fabulous selections from our award-winning wine list, which he helped create. We are indebted to these men for their hard work and dedication.

Our dining room runs superbly under the direction of Luis Saucedo, Mario Para, Benjamin Castrejon, and Javier Castro. Although he is no longer with Carlos', we toast Bruce Crofts, who was our first sommelier and who helped build our wine cellar to award-winning status. And thoughts of Carlos' would not be complete without remembering Karl Meyer. A special thanks to Don Yamauchi, Eric Aubriot, and Alan Wolf, talented chefs who added their own special style as they helped us during the early stages of writing this book. Thank you also to our pastry chef, Elizabeth Cedeño. Thanks to Harry Harrison, who works in our office and helps to keep the books (and our lives) straight. Special thanks to Toni Gramm, our office manager, who smiled through every assignment we gave her. We pushed her workload to the outer limits and she never complained.

We've been fortunate to have so many fine people in the "business" side of our restaurant world. We so appreciate Elliot and Roz Neuberg, and Ben and Debbie Neuberg and their staff. Thanks for believing in us. We miss Elliot and think of him often. Thanks to our accountant, Dick Shapiro, who has been with us since the beginning. Thanks to our fish purveyors, Bonnie and Roy Axelson, and our meat distributor, John Fraulini. To our wine purveyors, too numerous to mention, we toast to your good health and continued success. Jo and Tony Terlato and their sons have remained our good friends over the years, and they supply us with so many things that are as important as their fine wines. We also appreciate the service of the Glunz family and Larry Binstein, who supply us with fabulous specialty items.

Besides these terrific people, many businesses have contributed to Carlos' success over the years. We are grateful to Gordon and Carol Siegel of Crate and Barrel and to Williams Sonoma, Bloomingdale's, and Chef's Catalogue with Carla and Allan Kelson. And special thanks to the Silver Sea family for welcoming us into your kitchens. We have enjoyed cooking with you around the world. A big thanks to Maggie Holyn and Cindy Polster.

We can't thank our families enough. From the day he was born in 1978, our son, Adam Nieto, has brought great joy to our lives. Our longtime customers can remember Adam from the time he was a toddler following in his father's footsteps by working in so many parts of the operation — from the line in the kitchen, to passing out rolls, to bussing tables, to asking patrons how they were enjoying their dinners. Adam, who now manages our sister restaurant, Café Central, has matured into a man with great intelligence, kindness, and warmth. We are so proud that he has joined us in the business.

We fondly remember other relatives, too: my mother, Edie Mizel, a fabulous cook and baker; my father, Aaron Mizel, and his wife, Annie, who have added so much to our business and personal lives; the memory of Rose and Ed Mizel and Bertha and Joe Hirtenstein, the most special grandparents, who supported us in every way imaginable; my Tante and Uncie, Roberta and Jerry Hirtenstein, who are "number one" in our book; and my brothers Kenny, Bruce, and Richie, and their families. They give special meaning to the word "family." Carlos' family is just as supportive. Isarua and Guillermo Nieto, Victoria and Enrique Nieto, and their families are a delightful part of our lives. The older we get, the more we appreciate the meaning of family. To all of you, a special thanks for being the foundation of our lives! We are truly blessed.

And speaking of blessings, we are equally lucky in the "friends" department. Suzanne and Al Friedman and their family are our very best friends. We have great respect for their knowledge of the restaurant business and we truly value their support and love. Chicki and Baykar Tatosian are the kind of friends who make life complete. We would also like to thank Sandi and Bob Chatz, Jane and Michael Linderman, and Sparky and Randy Weil for their continued support. We'd also like to mention our friend Richard Cohen and his late wife, Jill; Sara Friedman, Donna and Terry McKay, Lesley and Eddie Shapiro, Phyllis Cretors and her late husband, Henry; and Laura Waldbart. We share many of the same passions. To Mira Fairstain, thank you for your professionalism and friendship.

To all of our cruising buddies, thanks for sharing the world with us. To my friends and trainers at the stables, thanks for being understanding when I had to work instead of ride.

To Jean Collins, Jane Peterson, and Dana Trotter, our "regulars" from our cooking classes, thanks for volunteering to test and edit our recipes in your kitchens. To our other testers, Paula Bacon, David Baldwin, Susie Conen, Phyllis Cretors, Sara Friedman, Debbie Goodman, Alton B. Harris, Debbi Klein, Maureen Kotler, George Koziol, Jana McDonough, Donna McKay, Esther Michlin, Darren Ringel, Marley Stein, Jerry Vrabel, Tom White, and Ellen Wynn, we appreciate your testing our recipes in your homes. Your insights were a big help.

We are extremely grateful to our agent, Lisa Ekus. It was *beshert* that Jimmy Seder fixed us up. She is well respected in the publishing world and we were lucky she took us under her wing. She introduced us to Ken Bookman, an extraordinary editor whose time and efforts enhanced each recipe. His ideas helped to create the format for the finished book. Lisa's diligence in finding the best home for this cookbook led us to our publisher, Gibbs Smith, and to our editor, Madge Baird, and associate editor, Melissa Barlow. They have been great to work with and have translated our vision for this publication into a beautiful reality.

And what would a fine cookbook be without exceptional photographs? Thanks to Eric Futran for his creative and artistic images.

And last, but not least, our thanks to Arlene Bronstein. There are no words to express our gratitude to you. Without your diligence and unwavering foresight, this book would never have been completed. Thank you from the bottom of our hearts.

As we look over this list, we are overwhelmed and grateful that so many fabulous people have filled our lives. If by some chance we have omitted a name that should have been here, please know that we are truly sorry — and that we'll mention you first in the sequel to this book!

— *Debbie Nieto*

INTRODUCTION

Carlos' opened in a Highland Park, Illinois, storefront on November 11, 1981, overcoming months of construction, personnel and financial setbacks. Since then, it has distinguished itself as one of only a handful of top-rated restaurants in the Chicago area. Of all our culinary achievements in our years on the Chicago food scene, I think the most important thing we've done is figure out how to make you feel comfortable in the world of top-quality food and wine. The way we look at it, if we make you feel comfortable in the restaurant, you'll also feel comfortable making our recipes at home. That's why everything we do is intended to enhance your comfort and enjoyment. We must be succeeding: a recent survey by the Zagat Guide reports that Carlos' is considered Chicago's *most* popular restaurant.

Carlos himself is probably the main reason. His story is inspirational. Carlos Nieto was neither a professional chef nor a restaurant man when he came to America in the late 1960s. He was a silversmith in his early twenties in Mexico City. While running an errand for a family business, he came to America and never left. To earn pocket money, he took jobs as a busboy and then a waiter in various restaurants. He fell in love with the restaurant business, he fell in love with me, and before long, both became permanent parts of his life. I married Carlos, fell in love with restaurants, and abandoned my plans to continue as a paramedic. It was quite a moment when those low-rung restaurant jobs led us to opening our own restaurant.

The restaurant has evolved and maintained its excellence, partly because Carlos Nieto distinguished himself as a superb judge of talent. He knew what he had to do to make not just a first-rate restaurant, but a first-rate restaurant that people would want to visit over and over. When we first thought about writing *Carlos': Contemporary French Cuisine*, we imagined a very elegant book. But the restaurant is more than that. Carlos' is elegant, but it is also accessible and comfortable. That combination is the soul of the restaurant and, we hope, of this book.

Carlos dedicated himself to building a brilliant restaurant from the front of the house while hiring talented chefs to take care of the back of the house. "I'm always re-inventing the restaurant," he says, and whether that means changing the menu, redecorating, or updating the cooking style, his goal is always the same: to reinforce in customers the sense that you're getting a special treat by visiting our restaurant.

It's my goal, too. Although I now spend a lot of my time at Café Central, our more casual sister restaurant in Highland Park, I still frequent Carlos'. I spend most of my time in the front of the house, dedicating myself to conveying the same message to customers — that any visit will be a special treat. I constantly work the floor and visit tables. Everywhere I go, whether to the bank, the supermarket, or Carlos' front door, I always encounter our customers and greet them warmly. Inside the restaurant, I do whatever I can to enhance a customer's visit — not just by greeting and chatting, but also by overseeing and coordinating the restaurant's design and décor.

The best part of the treat, of course, involves food. We call our food contemporary French cuisine, and it is constantly evolving. We adapt our menus to the whims of nature and of the seasons, but we never compromise on the quality of the food we serve. In any given week, it's fun to change based on the special things that come our way. Most of our patrons really appreciate the creativity involved in preparing and executing their meals, but a few of our guests like to order the same thing over and over again, and of course we try to accommodate their wishes. People's tastes change, and we find that our customers today are more amenable to red meat, cream, and butter. Although we have learned to be more sparing with all three, we have more latitude today to make the food experience a little more special.

Another part of the treat involves wine. We love wine and always wanted to make wine a significant piece of our restaurant. In the beginning, we had only fifteen wines. They were a well-chosen fifteen, but that tiny number was it. With the help of Bruce Crofts, our first sommelier, plus lots of worldwide tastings, auctions, and bartering, we now have one of the finest wine collections in the world, with 15,000 bottles, a staff that's rich in wine expertise, and a slew of awards, including the Grand Award from *The Wine Spectator*. But wine is more than an extensive list. It's respecting the bottles and the patrons. You would have to look long and hard before finding a staff better skilled at matching food and wine. Our sommelier, Marcello Cancelli, has used his knowledge of wine, his skill as a journalist, and a lively sense of humor to craft extremely useful wine notes that you'll find with many of the recipes in our book.

What may be the most visible part of dining at Carlos' is our warm atmosphere, the feeling you get the minute you walk into our restaurant. We jump through hoops to make sure that every customer feels like royalty. When we first designed the restaurant, we wanted maximum seating, but we also wanted to maximize our customers' comfort. We worked hard to make our small space as appealing and cozy as possible. You'll also feel comfortable because the air you breathe isn't rarefied. We won't impose upon you our notion of what makes a great dinner. You'll certainly get one, make no mistake about that. We've worked hard at honing our cooking, service, and hospitality skills, and we make sure that all those skills are there in abundance for you. But we've never forgotten that the people who walk through our doors know more than a bit themselves about cooking, service, and hospitality.

There's a lot of old-fashioned, unbridled joy in the air, and if this isn't what you expect from a four-star French restaurant, well, we relish being unpredictable. And that's even before we've started feeding you. *Carlos': Contemporary French Cuisine* is dedicated to re-creating the Carlos' Restaurant experience in your home. So I'd like to tell you about two of the regular things we do at Carlos' that make us different from other fine restaurants — and that have helped us craft these recipes to reflect our high standards while assuring you a dish you can make at home.

One is our cooking classes. These classes have evolved into monthly lunchtime events that have every participant leaving with a big smile and a full stomach. We think those smiles are smiles of anticipation at how our students will apply what they've learned in their own kitchens and dining rooms. Our students — around thirty for each class — are divided into two groups. One group walks straight back into our main kitchen while the other group heads upstairs to our pastry kitchen. And there, led by our executive chef and our pastry chef, our students-for-a-day watch as two savory dishes and one dessert are prepared. They watch, listen to the masters, ask a ton of questions, take notes, get printed recipes — and then they trade rooms and repeat the process.

Some of our students have attended every session since the classes began twelve years ago. They have been our best word-of-mouth advertising for a fun and informative afternoon. It's impossible to attend a class with a master chef and not walk away with a tip or two that you'll use over and over, with knowledge of an ingredient you had never before used, with a great sauce or fish technique, or with your eye on a new piece of kitchen equipment. But the best part is that you've witnessed the prepar-ation of world-class food that you *know* you can duplicate at home.

The proof comes a few minutes later, when all the students meet in the dining room and enjoy a three-course lunch of the dishes they've just learned. The plates are all empty when they go back to the kitchen.

One class we remember well was typical. For that class-luncheon, our two savory courses were Leek and Winter Squash Soup with Gruyère Crouton followed by Roulade of Dover Sole with Chanterelles and Pea Sprouts in a Lobster Basil Emulsion. Both are elegant and arrive at the table looking beautiful. And as you would expect in a top-quality restaurant, they include multiple elements, more elements than you might serve at home. But if you think about it, we *must* be able to place the finished dish before you just a few minutes after you order it. We accomplish that by having an array of garnishes and sauces that are already prepared. Once you have a supply of the basic "pantry items" and seek out the best ingredients possible, you, too, can prepare first-rate food for yourself, your family, and your guests.

As for those multiple elements, they're versatile enough to go with a lot of dishes. Consider the Gruyère Croutons from the soup course. They would be perfect with many other soups and salads and they can be prepared in minutes. So we encourage you to think in that direction. Our visitors all smiled knowingly when they watched our chef peel the skin off the sole in a single motion. It's a trick they'll use over and over, whether preparing this recipe or another. And that's something else about a fine restaurant kitchen: perhaps the most important ingredient in each of our recipes is *thought*. Do you have a favorite home recipe that you invented yourself and are especially proud of? Same thing. The ingredients and preparation are extremely important, but the main reason it's so good is that it's the result of thought. That's how it works at Carlos', where our dishes don't just magically happen. They're conceived, tested, tinkered with, tested again, perfected, tested yet again — the process is exhaustive, but nothing goes on Carlos' menu until that process plays out. Similarly, no recipe has gone into this book without the same exhaustive process, thereby taking all the guesswork and risk out of your cooking it.

Just as our luncheon classes are customer-oriented, so are our Monday wine dinners. Carlos' is very proud of its extensive wine list and wine cellar. A list and a cellar like ours mean that the patrons who visit our restaurant take wine as seriously as we do — seriously enough to know that wine is an important part of the meal and must be chosen as carefully as everything else that you consume from our table.

People like that have home wine collections of their own — good ones, too. And we encourage them to make the most of those wines. So while many restaurants view Mondays as a non-event, we treat Mondays as a special event. On that day, we waive our usual corkage fees and invite our guests to bring their own wine treasures to dinner — in other words, to literally bring part of their home into our restaurant. We'll make sure that the food we serve does justice to the wine you bring. Is that the tail wagging the dog? Maybe, but so what? We love wine, we love food, and we know that you do, too. So we'll make everything work together. If our regular menu doesn't offer the right dish or the right sauce for the wine you've brought, we'll make whatever alterations are necessary to concoct something that does. And you'll leave with a smile. Again, it will be a smile of anticipation, because you'll be armed with ideas of how to best use other wines from your home collection at your home dinners.

One of our regular customers provides a perfect example of how this works. She's a strict vegetarian, and it's always a challenge to come up with something new and exciting to fill her desires for a dish with exceptional flavors and textures. After she returned from a trip to Oregon's Willamette Valley, she brought in a bottle of 1998 Adelsheim Pinot Noir "Elizabeth's Reserve." Our chef created a Mushroom Fricassee with Asparagus and Truffles. She was delighted, and so were we. And if the wine could have spoken, it would have been happy too. The dish became a new item on our menu.

Our own enthusiasm comes back to us from our customers. Inspired by them, Carlos and I have traveled the world to gather experiences and recipes, and we're proud to share our collection with home chefs, whether they're experienced in gourmet cooking or newer and less facile, but nonetheless excited about learning new techniques in their own kitchens. We've worked hard to fill these pages with simple and easy-to-follow recipes so the home cook can re-create them and feel comfortable with the world of French cooking. It's our hope that home chefs will explore these recipes, use them with their own favorite ingredients, and bring superb meals to their own tables.

Bon appetit!

— *Debbie Nieto*

**Adam Nieto serving
Wild Mushroom Wontons
with Duck Reduction (page 34)**

INGREDIENTS & EQUIPMENT

Our mission in this book parallels our mission at Carlos' Restaurant: to make you feel comfortable with our level of excellence and to make preparing our dishes feel approachable. It really is easy. In fact, most of the recipes in this book are easy, even though a small number involve multiple segments and a large number of ingredients. The reason probably lies in the first rule of fine cooking: use the best possible ingredients. Kitchen skills will come in time, but all the skills in the world won't make up for mediocre ingredients.

Another important rule is to read the entire recipe before you do anything. That rule will serve you well. You'll not only know what ingredients you need to acquire but you'll also get an idea of how much time you'll need, how many tasks you'll do simultaneously, what can be done ahead, etc.

Navigating the recipes in these pages is straightforward. Most of the information you'll need is in each recipe. But here are a few helpful guidelines about some ingredients and some common tools and techniques. First, the ingredients:

Butter. We recommend that you use only unsalted butter. Sometimes it's essential, such as when making Clarified Butter. But usually, it's a way of giving you more control. Salt levels in butters vary, depending on butter quality, location, or both, and personal taste varies even more. So buy your butter with no salt. If you think the finished dish needs more seasoning, sprinkle on some more salt before you eat it.

Currant tomatoes. These are the smallest tomatoes available. If you can't find them, the next largest is a grape tomato. They should be a fine substitute, although you'll probably need to reduce the number you use.

Eggs. We use large eggs. In most cases, a variation won't matter much. But in larger quantities, or in baking, it might.

Garlic. Unless otherwise noted, garlic quantities are stated with medium cloves in mind. A head of garlic, of course, consists of large, medium, and small cloves. Compensate as you wish, guided also by your personal taste. *Never use already peeled garlic that is sold in grocery stores; it has virtually no flavor.*

Juiced vegetables. We use them a lot, probably more than most restaurants or cookbooks. We believe that vegetable juice is a marvelous way to incorporate powerful flavor into a finished dish. A juicer would make a good investment.

Parmesan cheese is used frequently, both here and in other cookbooks. We recommend the best, fresh, imported Parmigiano-Reggiano.

A FEW WORDS ABOUT EQUIPMENT

Ring molds. We use them constantly because there's no better way to get salads, beans, potatoes, vegetables, or whatever to obey your wishes — especially when those wishes are for a perfect circle. Our kitchen is loaded with ring molds of many diameters, ranging from about 2 to 4 inches, and heights, from about half an inch to 3 inches. But that doesn't mean you need to follow suit. You can use scraps of PVC pipe, empty tuna cans with their lids removed, or even nothing at all.

Mandoline. There's no better tool for slicing vegetables or other hard foods into the paper-thin slices that some recipes need. Like so many kitchen tools, you could spend lots of money on a feature-filled slicer, or you could get away with a very inexpensive model. That decision is yours. Whatever you get, using a mandoline is a skill like any other, so spend a bit of time practicing.

Fryers. Most restaurant kitchens use a deep-fat fryer that's really deep and heavy-duty. Oil is dangerous when it's hot and messy when it's cool, so it needs to stay right where you want it. You can do your deep-frying in a skillet, but make sure the skillet is heavy and high-walled. Remember, the foods you toss into hot oil are there to have their water content removed. And you know what happens to hot oil when water gets into it: it bubbles furiously. If you use a skillet, make sure there's room for that to happen.

Squeeze bottles. We use thin, opaque plastic bottles that have pointed tops. You can buy them with small covers or fashion your own from plastic wrap. One of our favorite tops is thin and pointy and is used in many beauty salons for applying hair color. Squeeze bottles allow us more control when using our sauces and oils for decorating our plates.

MANY OF THE RECIPES IN THIS BOOK ARE ACCOMPANIED BY NOTES FROM OUR SOMMELIER, MARCELLO CANCELLI

"In writing what we believe are the best wine matches for the recipes in this book," he says, "we followed very straightforward guidelines:

"First and foremost, we wanted to follow the spirit of this book and make the wine selections accessible — meaning as easy to work with and to find as the recipes and ingredients that precede them. There's no sense making wine recommendations that you can't find.

"Second, we followed the spirit of the restaurant itself. Even as a fine-dining restaurant in the Midwest, we always strive to make our customers comfortable, with no feeling of intimidation. We have always believed in fun in a dining setting. To that end, the wine choices presented in this book are geared to the home gourmand.

"We could have made things esoteric, but we chose to keep you, the reader, at ease. So take the advice in stride. Choose wines that truly please you and use our notes as a guideline, not a strict mandate.

"Mainly, never forget to improvise if you wish and to have fun! This is the spirit of Carlos' Restaurant."

garnishes can add visual excitement to any dish. It's so important at Carlos', that we think hard about the perfect garnish for every dish. With a little effort, you and your guests can enjoy this special touch at home. They look very fancy, but they're not very difficult to make.

Most of the garnishes that adorn Carlos' finished dishes are prepared in a deep-fryer, although a heavy, high-walled skillet would do the job, too. The restaurant prepares a wide assortment of food items for garnishing (as shown in the left and right photos above) — herb leaves, carrot strips, potato slices, seaweed and eggroll wrappers, and slices of lotus root. Many of these items are sliced on a mandoline, a countertop tool that can produce slices far thinner and more uniform than could ever be done with just a knife.

Garnish preparation, as with so many other cooking skills, benefits from practice. With practice, you'll learn the optimum thickness for each food item, the best frying time and temperature, how many pieces to prepare in each batch, and which items should start with a coating of flour.

Carrot knots (pictured in the photo at left) are a good example. Carlos' starts with long "logs" and uses a mandoline and knife to prepare long, thin strips. By hand, we tie a knot in each strip, dust the strip in flour to avoid burning, and

toss a few strips at a time into hot oil. The furious bubbling that you'll hear is the sound of water boiling away as it is pulled out of the vegetable. The strips are removed from the oil when the vegetable has become crisp but hasn't discolored.

Some garnishes, such as the pastry dome (shown in the center photo and on the front of the jacket of this book) are oven-baked, not fried. This dome, for example, began as a large sheet of butter-infused puff pastry that was cut into pieces with a lattice roller, brushed with egg wash to hold poppy seeds and black sesame seeds, shaped on an upside-down coffee cup, and baked in a hot oven until golden.

But the most important ingredient is thought. We consider the color, texture, and consistency of the dish before we choose its garnish. For example, for a custard, we might prepare a medley of potato slices, so the crisp and colored potato shards will contrast with the creaminess of the food.

AMUSE-BOUCHE

We're not sure who came up with the idea of serving an amuse-bouche, those tiny taste sensations that set the tone for the meal to follow, but we know they have become an important tradition at Carlos' and that our patrons eagerly anticipate the amuse-bouche that will begin their meal. They are always curious to see the creative way our chef decides to start off the dinner. Taking the term from its native French, an *amuse-bouche* (pronounced amyewz-boosh) is a food that will make your mouth smile. That's what we try to do with these tiny morsels.

We look forward to them, too, because we don't have to follow the regular menu. It's the part of the meal where the chefs enjoy the most freedom. Each of these tiny treats sets a positive tone for the meal ahead. The presentations are always unique and cause our patrons to "oooh" and "ahhh." They excite the brain, tease the eye, and always please the palate. They foster anticipation for the meal to come, and because they're unannounced, unordered, and free, they're a pleasant surprise.

Our amuse-bouche always reflect the season at hand. Fresh vegetables, a cut of meat, or a thin slice of fish can be used in a variety of ways to awaken the taste buds. We know these recipes will inspire you, as they do our chefs, to create your own take on the presentations and the final taste.

Although the portion sizes are very small in the restaurant, any of the recipes in this chapter can be doubled or even tripled to make a great appetizer or a complete entrée. People love to gather and try many different small, pop-in-your-mouth sensations. You could actually plan an entire meal around servings of these small treats. Look through the recipes and see how they inspire you to experiment with new and different ways of pleasing your family and guests.

Although the restaurant servings are too small to warrant wine accompaniments, if you turn any of these amuse-bouche into larger appetizer portions, you may indeed want an accompanying wine. You'll find suggestions with each recipe.

So here's to great beginnings. After all, you get only one chance to make a first impression. This chapter will allow that impression to make your guests' mouths turn up in a big smile.

amuse-bouche

the recipes

ASIAN TUNA WITH HERB SALAD 28

OVEN-DRIED TOMATO AND GOAT CHEESE NAPOLEON 31

SMOKED SALMON AND CUCUMBER ROULADE 32

WILD MUSHROOM WONTONS WITH DUCK REDUCTION 34

MACADAMIA NUT, GOAT CHEESE AND RED GRAPE STRUDEL 35

GRILLED PRAWN WITH PARSNIP CUSTARD AND MICROWAVE POPCORN SAUCE 37

POACHED QUAIL EGGS WITH SMOKED SALMON AND HOLLANDAISE SAUCE 38

BEEF CONSOMMÉ WITH SUMMER VEGETABLES AND SEARED BEEF 41

BEET AND SPARKLING CIDER SHOOTER WITH MALPEQUE OYSTERS 42

CHICKEN AND TARRAGON MANICOTTI WITH TOMATO SAFFRON CREAM 45

MUSHROOM AND TRUFFLE CAPPUCINO 46

PROSCIUTTO CELERIAC TERRINE 49

Asian Tuna with Herb Salad

This is a very free-form recipe, with the quantities and even the choice of ingredients flexible enough to suit your taste and the availability of ingredients. The important thing is to get the freshest, highest grade of tuna possible. That will ensure the finished dish is fantastic. We love this as an amuse-bouche or as a delicious appetizer.

TUNA:

1   pound loin of tuna, best grade possible
Salt and white pepper to taste
Ground coriander seeds to taste
Ground fennel seeds to taste
2   tablespoons canola oil, approximately, for searing fish

HERB SALAD:

½   cup chopped daikon sprouts or bean sprouts
¾   cup chopped Italian (flat-leaf) parsley
¾   cup chopped herbs of your choice

ASIAN DRESSING:

¼   cup soy sauce
¼   cup sesame oil
2   tablespoons sherry vinegar
2   tablespoons white wine vinegar
½   cup water
¼   cup sugar

FOR SERVING:

12 to 18 cilantro leaves, for garnish
¾   cup salmon caviar

MAKES 6 SERVINGS

Season both sides of the tuna with salt, pepper, coriander, and fennel. Pour canola oil in a medium-size smoking skillet over high heat. Sear the tuna on both sides, but do not cook all the way through; the tuna should still be rare inside. Refrigerate. When chilled thoroughly, cut the tuna into small cubes or dice.

Combine the Herb Salad ingredients. Then, in a separate bowl, combine the dressing ingredients, refrigerate the mixture, and shake well before serving. Lightly toss the salad with the dressing.

To serve: place a small amount of dressed herb salad in the center of each plate. Top the salad with the tuna, garnish with 2 or 3 cilantro leaves, and dot the plate with salmon caviar.

Wine Match: A wine for this dish needs good acidity to enliven the savory herbs and Asian ingredients. We suggest an unoaked Riesling from Alsace in France. This wine is full-bodied enough for the richness of the dish, with plenty of acidity and ample lemon, pear, and nectarine flavors. If you like just a little sweetness in your wine, choose a German Kabinett. A German Riesling would also work well.

Oven-Dried Tomato and Goat Cheese Napoleon

This beautiful amuse-bouche has delighted our customers for many years. It is easy to prepare and fun to assemble. At Carlos' we do a few things that you can skip at home — removing the tomato skin, using a pastry bag, and making our own balsamic vinaigrette and basil oil. If you prefer, keep the tomato skin on, use a plastic bag instead, or buy pre-made versions of either condiment. If you'd rather make this into finger food, just fill an endive leaf with the tomato mixture, or place a dollop of the mixture on a piece of garlic toast, and garnish with a sprig of parsley. This is the size to serve as an amuse bouche.

TOMATO FILLING:

2   large tomatoes, skin removed, cored, seeded, and quartered
Salt and freshly ground black pepper to taste
½   cup Balsamic Vinaigrette (page 210)
3   cloves garlic, sliced very thin
4   sprigs fresh thyme, leaves only
8   ounces goat cheese, crumbled
1   teaspoon tomato paste
White pepper to taste
1   teaspoon minced shallots
1   teaspoon chopped chives

FOR SERVING:

24   endive leaves (12 white and 12 red, if possible; otherwise, all white)
Thyme sprigs
Basil Oil (page 213), for garnish
Halved orange currant baby tomatoes or quartered grape tomatoes, for garnish

MAKES 6 SERVINGS

To make the Tomato Filling mixture: Place the tomato quarters on a foil-covered metal rack with sides (such as a rack you would use for cooling cookies). Lightly sprinkle the tomatoes with salt and pepper, brush them lightly with the Balsamic Vinaigrette, place a garlic slice on each piece, and lightly sprinkle with thyme. Bake in a preheated 150 degree F oven at least 6 hours, or until the tomatoes are shriveled (although they will not be totally dried out). If your range doesn't have a setting that low, set the oven to its lowest setting and bake about 2 hours, checking frequently. If your range has a pilot light, its heat might be sufficient, although you should check the tomatoes frequently.

Place the oven-dried tomatoes in the workbowl of a food processor fitted with the steel blade. Pulse until the tomatoes are minced. With the machine running, add the goat cheese and tomato paste, and process until smooth. Add the white pepper, shallots, and chives, and process until blended. Adjust seasonings and spoon the mixture into a pastry bag fitted with a medium-size star tip (see Note).

To serve: Use 4 endive leaves (either 2 white and 2 red, or 4 white) for each serving, and stack them on each of 6 serving plates in a spiral design, alternating the colors. Squeeze a dollop of the tomato mixture into the crevice of each leaf. Garnish with the thyme sprigs, and dot the plates with Basil Oil. Garnish with tomato halves or quarters.

Note: Spooning the tomato mixture into a pastry bag and squeezing it from there will give you maximum control; but if you don't have a pastry bag, use a plastic bag, cut off one corner, and squeeze the mixture through the hole.

Wine Match: This dish works well with either a white or a red wine. Complement the flavors with a Sancerre from the Loire Valley in France; its heady floral aroma is a perfect match. Or contrast the flavors with a light red, such as a Beaujolais or a Chinon from the Loire Valley. The cheese will help to soften the tannins in the wine and will leave your mouth filled with beautiful fruit flavors.

Tip: To remove the skin from a tomato, boil enough water to cover the tomato and place it in the boiling water for about 1 minute. Remove and immediately run the tomato under cold water. The skin will come off easily as you rub it with your fingers.

Salmon and Cucumber Roulade

Smoked salmon seems to be a staple of every French restaurant, and we serve it classically with toast points, chopped eggs, capers, and onions. However, we always like to try new ways to present salmon to our customers, and this recipe is one example. You can either buy basil oil and brioche, or prepare them yourself.

1 heaping tablespoon crème fraîche or sour cream

2 teaspoons finely chopped tarragon

1 teaspoon minced chives

3 ounces smoked salmon, cut into 6 thin slices

6 paper-thin slices peeled seedless cucumber

Pinch of white pepper

Salt and white pepper to taste

6 thin slices of Brioche (page 228, or store-bought) or challah, crusts removed, toasted, and cut into 12 triangles

Basil Oil (page 213, or store-bought)

MAKES 6 SERVINGS

Whisk together the crème fraîche, tarragon, and chives. Spread a thin layer of crème fraîche sauce over the salmon. Place 1 cucumber slice over top, sprinkle lightly with pepper, and roll up. Cut as necessary to make the ends even. Adjust salt and pepper if necessary (remember, the salmon may already be salty).

To serve: place a small circle of the crème fraîche sauce in the center of each serving plate, and place a salmon roulade in the center. Lay 2 triangles of Brioche to either side. Drizzle lightly with Basil Oil.

Wine Match: A glass of Champagne is the perfect match for this dish. It's lively and crisp and beautifully counters the briny, salty aspects of the smoked salmon. Look for a light version without too much yeastiness.

Tip: Paper-thin cucumber slices are best achieved with a mandoline.

Wild Mushroom Wontons
with Duck Reduction

Wontons are fairly simple to make, yet they can be a special treat. These days, you can buy the wonton skins in most grocery stores. This small dish is great for lunch or dinner, but remember that it needs to be prepared the day before serving. If you double this recipe, you can make it into an appetizer and serve your guests two wontons instead of one. At Carlos', we cut the wontons into circles, but you can serve them as squares. They'll be just as delicious.

FILLING:

2	tablespoons olive oil
1	small onion, finely chopped
1	clove garlic, minced
4	cups coarsely chopped wild mushrooms
1	cup duck stock or chicken stock
½	cup heavy cream

Salt and white pepper to taste

1½	teaspoons finely chopped fresh tarragon

SAUCE:

¼	cup olive oil
2	medium carrots, coarsely chopped
2	cloves garlic, chopped
1	large stalk celery, coarsely chopped
1	medium onion, coarsely chopped
½	cup cream sherry
1	cup red wine
1	cup duck stock or chicken stock
8	tablespoons (1 stick) unsalted butter, cut into 8 pieces

WONTONS:

8	wonton wrappers (store-bought)

Egg wash (1 large egg mixed with 1 tablespoon water)

FOR SERVING:

20	bok choy leaves
1	teaspoon dark sesame oil, plus a dash for garnish
1	tablespoon soy sauce

Salt and freshly ground black pepper to taste

10	scallions, green part only, cut into julienne strips
1	radish, cut into small dice
½	cup seeded and finely diced tomatoes
¼	cup finely chopped parsley

MAKES 4 SERVINGS

To make the filling: Heat the olive oil in a large skillet, add the onion and garlic, and cook over medium heat until translucent, about 3 minutes. Add the mushrooms and cook until all the liquid has evaporated. Add the stock and reduce, stirring occasionally, until almost all the liquid is gone. Add the cream, stir to blend, and cook until thickened. Season to taste with salt, pepper, and tarragon, and refrigerate until ready for use. You can make the filling up to 2 days in advance.

You can prepare the sauce a day in advance: Heat the olive oil in a large pot or skillet just until the oil smokes. Add the carrots, garlic, celery, and onion, and cook until brown but not burned. Add the sherry and wine, and cook until almost all the liquid has evaporated. Add the stock, bring to a boil, and cook until reduced by half. Strain the sauce through a fine sieve and chill until ready to serve. Reheat the sauce before serving and whisk in the butter a piece at a time. Stir well to combine.

To prepare the wontons: Bring about 2 inches of lightly salted water to a gentle boil in a wide, shallow pot. Brush the surface of one wonton wrapper with some egg wash, place 1 tablespoon of filling in the center, place a second wonton wrapper on top, and press around the edges to seal. Place the wontons in the boiling water and boil gently until they float to the top, about 1 to 3 minutes.

To serve: Toss the bok choy leaves with 1 teaspoon of sesame oil and soy sauce, and cook over high heat just until wilted. Season with salt and pepper. Place a small amount of the sautéed bok choy on a serving plate, and top with a wonton. Surround with a generous amount of sauce, then drizzle a small amount of sauce over the wonton. Combine the scallions and radish with the dash of sesame oil and an additional pinch of salt and pepper, sprinkle over each wonton, and surround with chopped tomatoes and parsley. (See photo on page 17.)

Note: Use any leftover wonton skins as a fried garnish. (See our garnishing guidelines on page 22.)

Wine Match: A Pinot Noir from California, especially one from the central coast, is the perfect complement to this amuse-bouche. One from New Zealand, such as Martinborough, would also be terrific. Choose a light, bright Pinot Noir that has a distinct cherry flavor and a profusion of aromas, as this will help balance the richness of the dish.

Macadamia Nut, Goat Cheese and Red Grape Strudel

This dish is very special to look at and relatively easy to prepare, but phyllo dough can become brittle. To avoid this, work quickly and brush the dough frequently with melted butter to keep it moist. Have all your ingredients ready to go. If the dough becomes brittle and starts to break, your end product probably won't look as perfect, but it will still be delicious.

2   sheets phyllo dough, 14 x 18 inches each

4   tablespoons (½ stick) unsalted butter, melted

16   macadamia nuts, finely chopped

6   ounces goat cheese, crumbled

28   red seedless grapes

½   teaspoon white sesame seeds, toasted

Vegetable-oil spray

Black sesame seeds

Basil Oil (page 213 or store-bought)

MAKES 8 SERVINGS

Preheat the oven to 400 degrees F. Moisten a dish towel, squeeze it to remove any excess water, place the damp cloth on the counter, and spread the sheet of the phyllo dough on the cloth. Working very quickly, brush the dough with some of the melted butter, then place the second sheet of dough on top of the first. Sprinkle the dough with the chopped nuts. Sprinkle the crumbled goat cheese only on the bottom half of the long side of dough, line up 12 of the grapes along the top border of the cheese, and sprinkle the dough with the white sesame seeds. Quickly roll up the dough, starting with the cheese end and moving up through the grapes. Squash as you roll, so you end up with a fairly smooth roll.

Cut the roll into 2-inch pieces. Spray a cookie sheet with vegetable spray and drizzle with a little of the remaining melted butter. Place in the preheated oven for about 2 minutes, or just until the pieces begin to brown. Remove from oven.

Cut the remaining 16 grapes in half. To serve, place a piece of strudel on each dinner plate and surround each with 4 grape halves. Sprinkle with the black sesame seeds and drizzle Basil Oil around the perimeter of plate.

Wine Match: This dish requires a light, piquant red wine — something a little spicy with lively acidity. A Barbera from Italy is perfect. We want it to have enough body to match the oily, rich nuts and the rich texture and flavor of the cheese.

Grilled Prawn with Parsnip Custard and Microwave Popcorn Sauce

We think this is one of the most unusual sauces Carlos' has ever served. Our chef loves microwave popcorn, so one day he experimented with a freshly popped bag. We never would have expected the explosion of flavor that came from that kernel of an idea, but we are sure glad it popped into his head. It is has become one of our personal favorites.

MICROWAVE POPCORN SAUCE:

1   package (3½ ounces) microwave popcorn

½   cup sugar

2   tablespoons red wine vinegar

1½   cups heavy cream

1   cup whole milk

Salt and freshly ground black pepper to taste

2   drops Tabasco sauce

PARSNIP CUSTARD:

Nonstick spray

2   tablespoons unsalted butter

2   medium parsnips, peeled and chopped

Salt and freshly ground black pepper to taste

3   large eggs

¾   cup heavy cream

GRILLED PRAWN:

1   tablespoon olive oil mixed with 1 tablespoon canola oil

8   large prawns, tails removed (see Note)

Salt and freshly ground black pepper to taste

8 pieces popped corn, optional garnish

Herb sprig of your choice, optional garnish

Crumbled vegetable chips, optional garnish

MAKES 8 SERVINGS

Prepare the popcorn according to package directions. Open the bag and let the cooked popcorn cool for 1 minute. Place a large saucepan over medium heat, add the sugar, and stir constantly to brown and liquefy. Pour in the popcorn and stir so that each piece is coated with the caramelized sugar. (Be careful: any unpopped kernels can pop when heated. These kernels add flavor to the sauce, so they shouldn't be removed.) Add the vinegar, stir, add the cream and milk, and increase the heat to bring the mixture to a boil. Continue stirring at a simmer for about 5 minutes.

Pour the hot sauce into a blender, cover with a damp dish towel, and hold the edges as you turn the blender on low. Listen as the kernels are chopped; when they are a finer consistency, turn the blender to high for a minute or two. Add the salt, pepper, and Tabasco sauce; process on high for 1 minute. Pour the sauce through a fine strainer into a clean pot. If you are not ready to serve the sauce, refrigerate it and reheat just before serving.

To make custard: Preheat oven to 350 degrees F. Spray eight (4-ounce) ramekins with nonstick spray and set them aside. Melt the butter in a medium saucepan over medium heat, and add the parsnips. Cook until the parsnips are soft and lightly brown, about 10 minutes. Purée the parsnips in a food processor and season with salt and pepper.

Whisk the eggs until frothy. Add the cream and the parsnip purée, and stir until well blended. Fill each of the prepared ramekins halfway, and place in a baking pan with enough water to come halfway up the sides of the ramekins. Bake in the preheated oven for 20 to 25 minutes, or until the centers are set. The custards are done when a toothpick inserted in the center comes out clean. Remove from the water bath and allow to cool slightly. To unmold, run a small knife along the inside rim of the ramekin and carefully pop the custard out onto a serving dish.

To prepare the prawn: Place the oil mixture in a heavy skillet and heat it well without burning it. Sauté the prawns in the hot oil until they are lightly browned on all surfaces, about 2 minutes total. Season with salt and pepper.

To serve: Place one custard in the center of each of eight small serving bowls. Top each custard with one grilled prawn, and surround with some popcorn sauce. Garnish with an herb sprig, a piece of popped popcorn, or sprinkle a few crumbled vegetable chips on top. This is good warm or cold.

Note: Prawns and shrimp, though similar, aren't identical; if you use shrimp, buy large ones.

Wine Match: When this dish pops into your mouth, it should be paired with a wine that will explode with a heady, floral taste. A Viognier from Santa Barbara or one from the Rhône Valley would work well. This type of wine is aromatic and has a complex flavor of nectarines, apricots, and peaches. The acidity of the wine helps break the richness of the popcorn sauce while enlivening the earthiness of the parsnips.

Poached Quail Eggs with Smoked Salmon and Hollandaise Sauce

This beautiful little dish features an appealing combination of flavors and textures. Quail eggs are available in many Asian markets and other specialty stores, but check the freshness dates before you buy them. You could make this with a regular hard-cooked egg, slice it while cool, and serve it as an appetizer. A drizzle of beet juice would add a splash of color.

VEGETABLE-OIL SPRAY

8　quail eggs

HOLLANDAISE SAUCE:

2　large egg yolks
1　tablespoon sparkling white wine
1½　to 2 tablespoons Clarified Butter (page 220)
Pinches of salt and freshly ground white pepper

FOR SERVING:

8　round slices smoked salmon, about 1 ounce each, made with a cookie cutter
2　teaspoons fresh lemon juice or to taste
3　drops Tabasco sauce
Caviar (any variety), optional
Chopped chervil or parsley, optional

MAKES 8 SERVINGS

Cut eight 6-inch squares of plastic wrap, spread them out on the counter, and spray them with vegetable oil. Gently crack open a quail egg and place a raw egg in the middle of each piece of plastic wrap, Then form a "purse" by twisting the four corners of plastic wrap together and tying with some string to seal. (You can do this up to a day in advance.)

To make the Hollandaise Sauce: Place the egg yolks in the top of a double boiler. Half-fill the bottom of the double boiler with water and bring to a simmer, whisking the egg yolks as the water heats. Add the wine and continue whisking. Small bubbles will break through, and then, with further whisking, they will dissolve and the sauce will take on a smooth consistency. Heat over the gently boiling water, removing from the heat as you continue whisking. The wine and the whisking will lighten your sauce. Sauce should be a pale, creamy yellow. (The total whisking time is less than 5 minutes.) Continue to heat and whisk. Don't leave the pot over the heat the whole time or the eggs might scramble.

Slowly add the Clarified Butter a bit at a time, whisking and seasoning with salt and pepper after each addition. Keep the sauce warm.

Place the eight egg packages in a pot of gently boiling water. Cook for 2 minutes, or until the egg looks white and cooked, carefully turning the packages in the water once during cooking. The yolk should be neither hard-boiled nor runny. Remove the egg packages from the water and place them in a bowl to cool for 1 minute. Using scissors, open each egg package.

To serve: In eight small bowls, place a salmon round in the bottom and place an egg in the center of each round. Add the lemon juice and pepper sauce to the warm hollandaise and whisk to blend. Add more lemon juice to taste. Drizzle each egg with hollandaise sauce, garnish with a bit of caviar on top, and, for color, sprinkle with a bit of chopped chervil or parsley.

Wine Match: This is such a versatile dish. We can picture it being served on the Côte d'Azur within sight of a gorgeous sunny beach. It can be an amuse-bouche, an appetizer, or a fabulous brunch. Our first thought is to match it with a Champagne because we like the contrast with the briny flavor of the salmon. It would also be great paired with a sparkling wine or a good rosé like Tavel from Provence. The rosé would bring a bright, aromatic touch to the experience.

Tip: You can use your favorite hot pepper sauce. Hundreds of brands are on the market, but, basically, they're all some combination of vinegar and hot peppers. Tabasco is the best known of the brands.

Beef Consommé with Summer Vegetables and Seared Beef

The chefs at Carlos' describe this simple little dish as "interactive," because the diner helps put it together before eating it. Even though it is served warm, it is a perfect start for a summer dinner, and, of course, you can serve it any time of the year. The consommé can be prepared a day in advance. You can use canned chicken broth instead of the stock, although if you do, you should cut back on the amount of salt that you use.

2   ounces beef tenderloin (in 1 piece)
Salt and freshly ground black pepper to taste
Olive oil
14   ounces lean veal or chicken
3   large egg whites and their shells
1   stalk celery, coarsely chopped
1   carrot, coarsely chopped
1   bay leaf
1   teaspoon fresh parsley, flat or curly
1   sprig thyme
12   peppercorns
¼   teaspoon salt
½   plum tomato, seeds removed, coarsely chopped
4   cups Veal Stock (page 226), cold

GARNISH:

1   small zucchini, cut into small balls or small dice
1   small yellow squash, cut into small balls or small dice
1   carrot, cut into small balls or small dice
24   edamame (boiled soybeans)

MAKES 6 SERVINGS

Season the beef tenderloin with salt and pepper, then sear the meat in an extremely hot, medium-size pan with a small amount of olive oil until the outside is almost charred. The middle should remain very rare. Wrap the meat in plastic and place in the freezer; it must get hard so you can cut it into thin slices. When the meat is frozen, cut it into 6 thin slices and refrigerate until serving time.

To make the consommé: Place the veal or chicken, egg whites, and eggshells in a food processor fitted with the steel blade, then add the celery, carrot, bay leaf, parsley, thyme, peppercorns, salt, and chopped tomato. Purée for about 30 seconds. (This soft mixture is called a "raft" because it will float in the cold Veal Stock as it clarifies the liquid. The raft is not eaten.)

Pour the cold Veal Stock into a medium pot, spoon in the raft, and stir. Place the pot on the stove over medium heat, stirring constantly until the stock comes to a gentle simmer. Stirring will keep the egg whites from sticking to the bottom, which would give it a burnt taste. Keep scraping the bottom of the pot. When the stock gets hot, stop stirring and continue to simmer for 1 hour. Let cool slightly.

Line a conical strainer with a coffee filter. Push aside the raft and ladle only the liquid into the strainer. Keep the strained liquid warm until serving. (You can make this the day before and keep it in the refrigerator.) Heat thoroughly before serving.

Place 2 of each of the balled vegetables, 4 edamame, and 1 thin slice of cold meat on a Chinese soupspoon. Place the spoon on a plate large enough to hold a small bowl or espresso cup of the consommé. Fill the cup only half full. To avoid sliding cups and spoons, place a doily on each plate. Tell your guests that when they're ready to eat, they should pour the contents of the soupspoon into the consommé and wait 1 minute until the liquid warms the vegetables.

Wine Match: Look for a red wine with plentiful fruit flavors to help lift the earthiness of the dish without overwhelming the delicate flavors of the consommé and tenderloin. A red Zinfandel with apple, raspberry, and cherry flavors and just a touch of peppery-ness is perfect. Many people err in thinking that red meat requires a heavy Cabernet; you do not need big power to create a powerful taste.

Tip: Be sure to use lean meat, which will clarify the stock. Although it sounds strange, chopping the eggshells into the mixture will also help clarify the consommé.

Tip: If this presentation is too fussy for your taste, serve the consommé with the vegetables and the beef all together in a pretty little bowl like in our photo. It will taste just as good.

Beet and Sparkling Cider Shooter with Malpeque Oysters

Traditionally, a "shooter" is made with whiskey or tequila. The name came from shooting your head back and tossing the drink to the back of your throat to get a quick high. Eventually, the term *shooters* became popular when they were made with oysters on the half shell. Now these little drinks are in vogue as an amuse-bouche or appetizer. There are many different versions, and this recipe has become a Carlos' favorite.

9   baby beets or 1 medium beet, red or golden, juiced to yield 1/3 cup (see Note) or fresh beet juice

⅔   cup apple juice

¼   cup fresh orange juice (if store-bought, it should be high-quality, unsweetened, unpasteurized juice)

1   tablespoon fresh lime juice

1¼ cups sparkling apple cider

½   teaspoon sea salt

8   Malpeque oysters (any readily available fresh oyster will do)

1   apple, diced, for garnish

MAKES 8 SERVINGS

Combine the juices from the beets, apples, oranges, and lime, and add the cider, which will cause foam to form on the top. Skim off this foam, add half the sea salt, stir gently, and refrigerate until ready to serve. Stir again just before serving.

To serve: Open the oysters with an oyster knife, or have your fishmonger open them for you, although they should not be opened more than a couple of hours before serving. Pour the contents of each shell in the bottom of a tequila or cordial glass. Spoon a portion of the juice mixture over each oyster. Place some of the diced apple garnish in each glass. Serve immediately.

Note: Juice the beets and apples in an electric juicer. The apples should first be peeled, cored, sliced, and seeded.

Wine Match: This dish comes with its own drink, but if you choose to have a wine as well, find the right combination of minerals, acidity, and high aroma. Look for a Semillon, either on its own or in combination with Sauvignon Blanc. The combination with the cider and the briny oyster will send your taste buds soaring.

Tip: Wear gloves when you cut the beets to keep your hands from getting stained; alternately, beet juice is sold in some health-food stores.

Tip: Although you can use non-pasteurized or non-filtered apple juice, use only fresh orange and lime juice.

Chicken and Tarragon Manicotti with Tomato Saffron Cream

Substitute lobster for the chicken in this recipe and it becomes an extra-special start to a meal. If you do so, use about 8 ounces of cooked lobster meat. At Carlos', we have used the stuffing over rigatoni and in ravioli, so try it over your favorite pasta. For an amuse-bouche, you can use one manicotti and cut it into 4 pieces or stuff 3 rigatoni and create a pasta teepee.

8	large manicotti
¼	cup olive oil
1	carrot, peeled and cut into small dice
½	medium red onion, peeled and cut into small dice
1	medium fennel, bulb halved, stem cored, cut into small dice
1	boneless, skinless chicken breast half, cut into small pieces
1	tablespoon chopped tarragon
1½	cups heavy cream

Salt and freshly ground black pepper to taste

2	tablespoons unsalted butter
¼	cup white wine
1	tablespoon demiglace (optional)
1	large egg

SAUCE:

1	tablespoon olive oil
3	plum tomatoes, coarsely chopped
1	cup chicken stock
1	shallot, coarsely chopped
5	fresh basil leaves
¾	cup heavy cream

Pinch of saffron

1	teaspoon salt
1	teaspoon pepper

FOR SERVING:

1	tablespoon olive oil

Micro greens, optional garnish
Fried leeks, optional garnish
Celery leaves, optional garnish
Fennel fronds, optional garnish

MAKES 8 SERVINGS

Cook the manicotti in a large pot of rapidly boiling water according to the package directions, or until a little more cooked than al dente. Drain and toss with 1 tablespoon of the olive oil to keep the pieces from sticking together.

Place the remaining olive oil in a large saucepan, heat the oil until it's very hot, then sauté the diced vegetables, stirring constantly, until they are wilted but not browned. Add the chicken pieces to the sautéed vegetables and stir, cooking until the chicken pieces are white and cooked through. Add the tarragon and cream, stir, and then add the salt and pepper. Add the butter and continue stirring until the mixture comes to a boil. Cook for about 10 minutes, add the wine, and cook 5 minutes more. If desired, add the demiglace to the chicken, stir until it melts, and cook 2 minutes more. The liquid will be tan. Remove pan from the heat and let cool. Add the egg to the cooled chicken and stir to combine. (The egg will bind the chicken together so it won't fall out of the manicotti.)

To make the sauce: Heat the olive oil in a medium saucepan over high heat. Add the tomatoes and chicken stock, and bring to a boil, cooking until the stock has been reduced by half. Add the shallot and basil, cook for about 2 minutes, and add the cream. Stir to combine, add the saffron, and stir again. Add the salt and pepper and cook for 10 to 15 minutes, until the sauce is reduced by half. Strain the tomato mixture through a fine sieve.

To serve: Stand one piece of manicotti on its end on each of eight serving plates and stuff the manicotti pieces with the chicken mixture. Place the oil in a hot, medium-size pan, then sauté the stuffed manicottis, two at a time, until they are crispy. Place one finished manicotti on each of the eight serving plates, and diagonally swoop the sauce across the manicotti. If desired, garnish the plates with micro greens, fried leeks, celery leaves, or fennel fronds.

Wine Match: The tomato and saffron hold the key to a successful wine match. We need a wine with refreshing acidity and good minerality but without exuberant fruit flavors. A good Macon-Villages, a Chardonnay from Burgundy in France, works beautifully.

Tip: To make small dice from vegetables, first cut them into thin strips, then turn them sideways and chop.

Tip: Avoid stinging eyes when chopping onions by first washing your knife in cold water.

Tip: Give your stuffing some zest by stirring in a drop or two of Tabasco sauce.

Mushroom and Truffle Cappuccino

This dish is perfect for a cold winter day. It really warms up the appetite for the meal to follow and it looks beautiful served in a small espresso cup. The foam on top makes it an unusual way to start a dinner. This recipe is also perfect as a creamy mushroom soup for 4 people, so consider it as a larger first course. It is also delicious as a sauce over goat-cheese ravioli. Drizzle it with truffle oil and a sliver of fresh truffle for a fabulous finish.

2 tablespoons unsalted butter

1 leek, white part only, halved lengthwise, cut in ½-inch slices, rinsed thoroughly, and drained

6 large shallots, peeled and thinly sliced

6 chanterelle mushrooms, cleaned and sliced

10 shiitake mushrooms, cleaned and sliced

6 crimini mushrooms, cleaned and sliced

⅔ cup Port wine

1 cup chicken stock

1 bouquet garni made with 10 peppercorns, 2 bay leaves, 14 thyme sprigs (see Note)

2 cups heavy cream

1 teaspoon salt

¼ teaspoon white pepper

Skim-milk foam (see Note)

Porcini mushroom powder, store-bought

8 small pieces truffle, for garnish

Truffle oil

Chive spears, optional garnish

MAKES 8 SERVINGS

Melt the butter in a large pan. When the butter begins to brown, add the leek and shallots to the pan, and toss to coat with the butter. Cook over medium heat for about 5 minutes, or until the vegetables are wilted. Add the mushroom slices, stir to combine, and cook over medium heat, stirring frequently, until the mixture is lightly browned, about 10 minutes. (Any little brown bits clinging to the pan are called "fond," and will add flavor to the final liquid. Those bits will become part of the liquid when you deglaze the pan.)

Add the wine. (Be careful. The alcohol can start to flame if it touches the burner.) Cook, stirring, for 2 to 3 minutes, until reduced by half. Add the chicken stock, continue stirring, and bring to a boil. Add the bouquet garni, and cook until the mushrooms are very tender, about 10 to 15 minutes. Remove the bouquet garni.

Place the hot vegetables and liquid in a blender. Add half the cream, blend, and slowly add the rest of the cream until the mixture is smooth and creamy. Add salt and pepper, blend again, and adjust seasonings to taste. Pour the liquid through a fine strainer into a clean pot, and bring the liquid to a simmer.

Fill eight warmed espresso or demitasse cups with soup until the cups are three-quarters full. Place a dollop of the skim-milk foam over the soup in each cup, and lightly sprinkle with some porcini powder (this looks like cinnamon).

Garnish each cup with a small slice of truffle placed in the center of the foam. Drizzle a few dots of truffle oil atop the cup, and, if you wish, place a few small chive spears into the liquid.

Note: Make a bouquet garni by placing the peppercorns, bay leaves, and thyme on a double-layered square of cheesecloth. Roll up the cheesecloth like a cigar and secure with twine.

Note: Create skim-milk foam with an espresso machine or a hand-held frother. Alternatively, you can whip a small amount of heavy whipping cream until it's foamy.

Wine Match: Although a Pinot Noir is always a good choice for a dish with great mushrooms, the truffles here make one want to sip a Nebbiolo from Italy's Piedmont region, where truffles are so plentiful. The rich, earthy flavor of the mushrooms and truffles contrast with the bright acidity and are matched by the great truffle aroma of this type of wine.

Tip: When you use your blender, remove the little plastic piece in the middle of the top (or remove the entire top) and cover with a damp dish towel. This allows the steam to escape. Otherwise, steam can build up and cause the contents to explode.

Prosciutto Celeriac Terrine

Celeriac is the French word for celery root. It's common in many of France's favorite dishes, and this dish would certainly be a favorite. It combines many textures in both presentation and taste. You'll need some mayonnaise to hold the celery root slices together, but if you cut down on the quantity, it will still taste great; it will just be a little less creamy.

1   leek, peeled to the core until its circumference is about that of your thumb
1   medium celery root, peeled and sliced into very thin julienne (see Note)
1   cup mayonnaise, a bit less if you wish
1   teaspoon black sesame seeds
3   ounces prosciutto, sliced paper-thin
Salt and freshly ground black pepper to taste
Micro greens, optional

MAKES 8 SERVINGS

Place the peeled leek, bending it if necessary, in a pot of boiling water for about 5 minutes, or until it is soft and cooked through. Remove the leek from the boiling water and plunge it into ice water to stop the cooking. Place the julienned celery root in a large mixing bowl, add the mayonnaise, and stir to coat. Add the black sesame seeds and stir to combine.

Line a small terrine mold with plastic wrap, then line the terrine with the prosciutto slices, overlapping the slices by half to three-quarters. (The plastic wrap should be a large enough piece so that it can form a seal when folded over the top of the terrine.) Place the celery root mixture in the bottom of the terrine. It should come about a quarter of the way up. Cut off the bottom of the leek and place the whole leek on top of the celery root mixture. Top with more of the celery root mixture, and season with salt and pepper. (Consider the saltiness of the prosciutto as you judge the amount of salt to add.) Top with a layer of prosciutto, and fold the overlapping prosciutto slices over the top. Pack tightly, pushing down on the top layer of prosciutto. Fold over the plastic wrap to seal the terrine, and place a heavy weight directly on the terrine. (Use pie weights or a can of soup, for example.) Refrigerate the terrine for at least 2 hours.

To serve: Remove the terrine from the refrigerator. Through the plastic wrap, cut the terrine into 1-inch slices, using a serrated knife. Remove the plastic, and place one slice on each of the eight serving plates. Garnish with micro greens, if desired.

Note: To get uniformly thin slices, use the julienne blade on a mandoline. You want your final yield to be approximately 2 cups, packed. Don't have a mandoline? Use a julienne blade in a food processor or use a box grater.

Wine Match: To enliven this dish and contrast with the saltiness of the prosciutto, a light Pinot Grigio is great. The aromatics of this wine contrast with the earthiness of the recipe's ingredients. We also want to complement the simplicity of this preparation with an uncomplicated wine.

Tip: Don't have a terrine mold? Use a piece of PVC pipe or another container that can support a bit of weight.

APPETIZERS

Many of our regulars love our dining room's rare combination of elegance and intimate warmth. Even before the menus arrive, the atmosphere of the restaurant itself serves as an appetizer to the meal. Rarely do our patrons pass on an appetizer. Most of them find it the perfect way to begin their culinary adventure, especially when it contrasts with the entrée that will follow.

We like our selection of appetizers to be diverse and inviting, and even though the selection changes all the time based on the season at hand, we are still glad to prepare some of our customers' special requests if they call us a day or two before they arrive. Two of our favorite customers have been coming to Carlos' since we opened our doors in the early 1980s. They always want our escargots with Roquefort sauce and brioche. When we see their name in our reservation book, we know to have that dish ready for them.

We have offered you recipes for some of our most requested appetizers. The Crab Tower with Balsamic Vinaigrette has been featured in many magazine and newspaper articles. It is beautiful to look at and delicious to taste. The Foie Gras with Apples, Grapes, and Peppercorn Beurre Rouge Sauce combines a traditional French taste with a newer appeal. In fact, you can't go wrong with any of our appetizers. They are a wonderful way to begin your meal, whether you are in our dining room or your own. We toast to you and all your beginnings.

appetizers
the recipes

AUTUMN VEGETABLE RISOTTO WITH PARMESAN TUILE 55

LOBSTER NAPOLEON 56

CRAB TOWER WITH BALSAMIC VINAIGRETTE 58

LOBSTER RISOTTO MILANESE 60

SMOKED SALMON AND GOAT CHEESE FRITTATA 61

MUSHROOM FRICASSEE WITH ASPARAGUS AND TRUFFLES 63

MARINATED SQUAB WITH SPINACH AND TOMATOES 64

FOIE GRAS WITH APPLES, GRAPES AND PEPPERCORN BEURRE ROUGE SAUCE 66

ROASTED VEGETABLE TERRINE WITH ROASTED GARLIC-CARROT SAUCE 68

BRUSCHETTA WITH TOMATO, GOAT CHEESE AND BASIL 71

Autumn Vegetable Risotto with Parmesan Tuile

This creamy risotto is a perfect complement to the autumn vegetables. Substitute another autumn vegetable if one of these is not available, or increase the quantity of one or more of the others. This dish is flexible enough that you can make it any time of year. The tuile is a flat, textured, cookie-like presentation that's surprisingly easy to prepare but looks quite impressive. You'll use it to garnish many other recipes. In the photo we sprinkled it with black sesame seeds.

TUILES AND VEGETABLES:

4 to 6 tablespoons grated Parmesan cheese
1   tablespoon oil (any combination of olive oil and canola oil), divided
½   butternut squash, peeled and cut into small dice
1   small chayote squash, cut into small dice
1   small zucchini, cut into small dice
1   small yellow squash, cut into small dice
½   small spaghetti squash, seeds removed

RISOTTO:

½   cup olive oil (or combination of olive oil and canola oil)
1   small onion, finely diced
2   medium shallots, minced
3   cloves garlic, mashed
10   ounces uncooked arborio rice
¾   cup white wine (dry or sweet)
2   quarts warm chicken stock, approximately

TO SERVE:

2 to 3 tablespoons unsalted butter
1   tablespoon minced chives
1   small shallot, minced
¼   cup heavy cream
⅓ to ½ cup grated Parmesan cheese
Salt and freshly ground black pepper to taste
1½   tablespoons honey, optional
Basil Oil (page 213), for garnish
8   fried sage leaves (page 22), for garnish
4   fresh thyme sprigs, for garnish

MAKES 4 SERVINGS

To make the tuiles: Warm a small nonstick skillet and place a 2- to 3-inch ring mold in the middle. Sprinkle enough Parmesan cheese inside the ring to form a thin layer. When the cheese begins to melt and turn light brown, quickly place the hot pan on a bed of ice. The cheese will instantly harden and lift off. Repeat three more times. (You can do this without ring molds. Simply sprinkle the cheese in a freeform circle, or cover the entire bottom of the pan and break the resulting large tuile into smaller pieces to make delicious "crisps." Set the finished tuiles aside on paper towels.)

To prepare the vegetables: Preheat oven to 350 degrees F. Heat 2 teaspoons of the oil in a large skillet and sauté the butternut squash and chayote squash until fork-tender, about 5 minutes. Add the zucchini and yellow squash and cook another 3 to 5 minutes. Set aside to cool. Coat the spaghetti squash half with the remaining oil, then roast in the preheated oven for about 20 minutes. Remove from oven, let cool completely, and, using a fork, "pull" out the insides and cut into small pieces. Set aside.

To make the risotto: Heat the oil in a large pan, and sweat the onion, shallots, and garlic in the hot oil until transparent. Add the rice and cook for 2 minutes, stirring constantly to avoid burning and to coat each grain of rice with the oil. Keep stirring and add the wine. Reduce by half over medium heat for approximately 5 minutes. Add the stock to the rice a half cup at a time. Add more stock only after the rice absorbs the stock in the pan. Keep stirring and adding stock until the rice is al dente, approximately 20 minutes. You may not need all of the stock.

To serve: When the risotto is finished, reduce the heat and add the vegetables, butter, chives, shallot, cream, and grated cheese, and cook until the mixture is creamy but not loose — to the consistency of oatmeal. Adjust salt and pepper, and add the honey, if desired. Spoon the risotto into four large bowls. Surround each with a light ring of Basil Oil and garnish with 2 sage leaves and 1 thyme sprig. Press one Parmesan tuile so it stands up in the center.

Wine Match: With so many vegetables in this dish, the wine should balance their flavors and textures. A Pinot Gris embellishes the richness of this risotto. A wine from the Alsace region is perfect. It has good acidity and lovely wildflower aromas with subtle fruit and independence from oak.

Tip: For everyday serving at home, dispense with the three garnish ingredients at the end of the recipe. The color of the vegetables will make an attractive presentation.

Lobster Napoleon

We conceived this recipe on the beach in St. Tropez after dining at a restaurant called Club 55. The atmosphere was casually elegant and the food was beyond compare. We wanted to bring a taste of our south-of-France experience back for our patrons. This is an exceptional appetizer in terms of both taste and presentation. Prepare the dressing a day in advance to let the herbs and spices blend. In larger portions, this could serve four for a special summer lunch entrée.

DRESSING:

- ⅓ cup crème fraîche
- 2 tablespoons regular mayonnaise
- ½ small red onion, minced
- 1 plum tomato, seeded and cut into small dice
- 1 tablespoon chopped fresh tarragon
- 1 teaspoon Dijon mustard
- 1 tablespoon finely chopped chives
- ½ teaspoon fresh lime juice
- ½ teaspoon ground cumin
- ¼ teaspoon celery salt
- ½ teaspoon Roasted Garlic Purée (page 222)

Pinch of cayenne pepper

Salt and freshly ground black pepper to taste

- ½ teaspoon small capers, drained

NAPOLEON LAYERS:

- 6 sheets (14 x 18 inches) frozen phyllo dough
- 8 tablespoons (1 stick) unsalted butter, melted
- ½ cup chopped fresh tarragon (or more to taste)

MAKES 4 SERVINGS

Combine the dressing ingredients in a medium bowl. Refrigerate for 1 to 2 days.

To make the Napoleon layers: Preheat the oven to 350 degrees F. Place 1 sheet of the frozen phyllo dough on a parchment-lined jelly roll pan and lightly brush with some of the melted butter. Top with a second phyllo sheet and brush the second sheet with more of the melted butter. Sprinkle lightly with some of the chopped tarragon. Top with a third sheet, brush with additional melted butter, top with a fourth and fifth sheet, brushing each with additional melted butter. Sprinkle the fifth layer with more of the tarragon, top with a sixth sheet, and brush with more melted butter.

Quickly cut the cold phyllo layers into eight triangles, approximately 3 x 2 x 2 inches. (You should have enough to make a few extra triangles. Do so. They're very delicate and can break or crumble easily.) Brush some melted butter on another sheet of parchment paper, this one large enough to cover the phyllo triangles, and place the parchment on the phyllo, buttered side down. Press lightly with another jelly roll pan and leave the pan on top for its weight.

Bake for approximately 10 minutes. Rotate the pan 180 degrees and bake for approximately 5 minutes more, or until the triangles are golden brown. Remove the triangles from the jelly roll pan and place on paper towels to remove any excess butter. (This recipe may be made one day in advance, but if you're not using it right away, do not store the phyllo in the refrigerator. Rather, store in an airtight container between layers of paper towel.)

To serve: combine half of the sour cream and the tarragon in a small bowl. Set aside. Form 3 concentric circles on each of 4 large dinner plates. Make the outer circle by spooning a thin ring of the sour cream–tarragon mixture around the border of each plate. Make the middle circle by sprinkling chopped egg white. And make the inner circle by sprinkling

½   cup sour cream, divided
1   tablespoon minced fresh tarragon
1   hard-cooked egg, white and yolk
    separated and finely chopped
2   tablespoons minced chives
½   small red onion, minced
Freshly ground black pepper to taste
16 small capers
16 leaves baby spinach
2   tablespoons olive oil, divided
32 leaves Italian (flat-leaf) parsley
4   lobsters, about 1 pound each,
    steamed or boiled, chilled, and
    meat removed from tail, knuckle,
    and claw
1   plum tomato, seeded, quartered,
    most of the meat removed, and
    finely diced
1   ounce caviar

chopped egg yolk. Next, sprinkle each plate with chives, red onions, and black pepper. Then dot each plate with 4 capers.

In a small bowl, mix the spinach with half of the olive oil and stir to lightly coat the leaves. Place 4 leaves in the center of the plate. Mix the parsley leaves with the remaining olive oil and place 8 moistened leaves on top of the condiment circles.

Cut the lobster meat into bite-size pieces. Add the diced tomato and the reserved dressing, and stir to evenly coat the lobster. Place a small portion of the lobster mixture on the dressed leaves and top with a baked phyllo triangle. Top with another dab of the lobster mixture, then cover with a second phyllo triangle, placed in the opposite way of the first. Decorate the top of the phyllo with a small piece of coated lobster in the center and 2 dabs of the remaining sour cream on either side. Dot the top with additional sour cream and some caviar.

Wine Match: This dish almost begs for a crisp white Burgundy to enhance the rich, ample flavor of the lobster. A Chassagne-Montrachet leaps to mind with its "fatness" (which is wine talk for its rich, ample, mouth-filling flavor). The minerality of the wine contrasts with the richness of the dish, yet honeyed, creamy notes perfectly complement the lobster. Yum!

Tip: For simpler serving at home, dispense with any of the three concentric circles of garnish, the parsley, or the spinach.

Crab Tower with Balsamic Vinaigrette

This appetizer was created as a special Mother's Day surprise, and it is absolutely beautiful. In fact, it later appeared on the cover of *North Shore* magazine and quickly became one of Carlos' signature offerings. Your guests will think you spent hours preparing this dish. Let them think so — even though it's actually easy. For a summer luncheon, you could place this "tower" in the center of mixed greens and drizzle them with the balsamic dressing. Serve it with some warm cheese straws or fresh French rolls, add a fabulous dessert, and you'll have a complete meal.

6 to 8 ounces jumbo lump crabmeat, picked clean and chopped
1   seedless cucumber, peeled and finely diced
5   plum tomatoes, seeded and diced
¼   teaspoon extra-virgin olive oil
1   teaspoon minced cilantro
¼   teaspoon lime juice
Salt and freshly ground black pepper to taste
2   teaspoons crème fraîche

VINAIGRETTE:

¼   cup balsamic vinegar
¾   cup extra-virgin olive oil
1   tablespoon chopped shallots

GARNISH:

2   tablespoons chopped scallions (green part)
16   small sprigs chervil, for garnish

MAKES 4 SERVINGS

Place the crabmeat in a medium bowl. Combine the prepared cucumbers and tomatoes in a second medium bowl, add the ¼ teaspoon of olive oil, and toss gently. Blend in cilantro, lime juice, salt, and pepper. Drain any liquid from the chopped crabmeat, and stir in the crème fraîche and additional salt and pepper, if desired.

To make the vinaigrette: Combine the vinegar, the ¾ cup of olive oil, shallots, and additional salt and pepper.

To serve: Center a 2-inch ring mold on each of four serving plates. Place one-quarter of the crabmeat in the ring, top with one-quarter of the cucumber-tomato mixture, and top with a quarter of the scallions. Remove the ring and garnish with a few small sprigs of chervil. Whisk the balsamic dressing, and drizzle over the crabmeat for each serving.

Wine Match: Ride the popularity of New Zealand wines by choosing a Sauvignon Blanc with its crisp acidity and minerality to contrast with the richness of the crab and yet create a zing with the sharpness of the cilantro.

Lobster Risotto Milanese

We're constantly traveling the world in search of new and exciting taste sensations. This appetizer came from one of our culinary tours to Italy. You may wonder how an Italian recipe fits in a French restaurant. In fact, many of the best French recipes have an Italian or "Neapolitan" influence. This recipe takes at least 45 minutes to prepare, but it's well worth the time. It's so rich and delicious that you could consider serving it as a luncheon entrée accompanied only by a small green salad. Its creamy texture makes it perfect for a winter affair.

2	lobsters, about 1 pound each (see Note)
½	cup olive oil
1	small onion, finely chopped
2	medium shallots, minced
3	cloves garlic, minced
1½	cups uncooked arborio rice
16	saffron threads
¾	cup white wine
4	drops Tabasco sauce
2	quarts lobster stock or clam juice, approximately
¾	teaspoon salt or to taste
2	tablespoons unsalted butter
¼	cup heavy cream
2	tablespoons chives
½	cup grated Parmesan cheese
½	teaspoon black pepper

MAKES 4 SERVINGS

Steam the lobsters for 5 minutes and plunge them into ice water to stop the cooking. Remove all the meat, slice the claw meat into narrow strips, and dice the rest. Set aside.

Heat the olive oil in a 4-quart pot and sauté the onion, shallots, and garlic in the hot oil until translucent, about 2 to 3 minutes. Make sure the garlic doesn't burn, although it's fine for it to turn light brown. Add the rice and stir constantly to coat each grain and prevent burning. When the oil has been absorbed, add the saffron, wine, and Tabasco sauce. Stir constantly over medium heat to reduce the liquid by half, approximately 10 minutes.

Heat the stock and keep it warm throughout the entire preparation. Add ½ cup of stock to the rice and stir constantly until the stock has been absorbed. After about 5 minutes, add ½ teaspoon of the salt. Continue adding stock in small quantities until the rice is softened but still firm. You may not need all the stock.

When the risotto is the consistency of loose oatmeal, reduce the heat and add the diced lobster meat, butter, cream, chives, and grated cheese. Add the pepper and remaining salt. Cook until creamy. Serve in small bowls, topped with the sliced lobster claws.

Note: You can substitute 3 lobster tails and 2 claws prepared by a fishmonger.

Wine Match: It's important to choose the wine for this dish based on the combination of spices, the richness of the lobster, and the creaminess of the risotto. So even though the Chardonnay-lobster combo comes to mind, the saffron dictates that you stay away from oaky wines. If you want to be adventurous, seek out a Southern Italian beauty called Fiano d'Avellino. It's an exotic marriage.

Tip: Two things to remember when you make risotto: first, don't let the risotto get too dry (add more liquid after the previous addition has been absorbed). Second, never let risotto come to a boil or it will separate.

Smoked Salmon and Goat Cheese Frittata

Although we serve this dish as an appetizer, we also like to make it at home for breakfast or brunch. Here's a tip: find a fabulous bread to serve with it. At Carlos', we have great French-bread rolls that are crunchy on the outside and moist and light on the inside.

6   large eggs
¼   cup heavy whipping cream
2   tablespoons chopped chives
Salt and freshly ground black pepper to taste
¼   cup water
2   drops Tabasco sauce
1   tablespoon olive oil
2   scallions, finely chopped (keep the white and green parts separate)
1   clove garlic, minced
1   tablespoon unsalted butter
3   ounces smoked salmon, cut into ¼-inch strips
3   ounces goat cheese, crumbled
Mixed green salad with light herb or Roasted Red Pepper and Dill Dressing (page 212), optional

MAKES 4 SERVINGS

Preheat oven to 350 degrees F.

Whisk the eggs in a medium mixing bowl, add the heavy cream and whisk again. Add the chives, salt, pepper, water, and Tabasco sauce, and whisk a third time. Place the olive oil in a heavy 9-inch nonstick ovenproof skillet, and sauté the chopped white part of the scallions in the hot oil over medium heat. As the scallions begin to sweat, add the garlic and butter, and continue to sauté.

Reduce the heat to low, add the smoked salmon, and toss, just to warm. Whisk the egg mixture again and add it to the pan. Cook on the stovetop using a "scrambled eggs" motion, moving the eggs off the bottom of the pan, cooking through all the ingredients. When eggs begin to set, top them with the scallions and three-quarters of the goat cheese. Place in the preheated oven for approximately 15 minutes, or until eggs are firm. (Watch carefully as the sides of the eggs may rise and begin to brown. If that happens, cover eggs lightly with foil and continue cooking until done.)

Remove the pan from the oven and let stand for 1 minute. Run a knife around the edge of the pan and loosen the eggs by sliding a spatula under them. Place the eggs on a large heated serving plate, cut into four wedges, and place a wedge off-center on each of four separate dinner plates. Sprinkle with the remaining goat cheese. If desired, serve with some mixed green salad.

Wine Match: We recommend a fruity white wine such as a Vouvray from France to contrast nicely with the smoky, salty ingredients in this dish, providing the refreshing taste that it needs. If you serve this as a brunch treat instead of as a traditional appetizer, a sparkling wine or a Pinot Blanc is a perfect pairing.

Tip: If you'd like the eggs to have a fluffier texture, whip the cream before adding it to the eggs, then fold in the other ingredients.

Mushroom Fricassee with Asparagus and Truffles

This recipe is designed for the true mushroom lover. It is so quick and easy that you might use it as a frequent side dish. Truffles are more readily available than ever before, and the tiniest piece adds the greatest taste. Remember, you can use any wild or exotic mushroom that's available. In our photo we placed the mushroom fricassee in a potato basket.

4   teaspoons olive oil, divided
1   pound wild mushrooms (any variety in any combination), cleaned, trimmed, squeezed to remove excess moisture, and halved or quartered
12   green asparagus tips, cleaned and trimmed to 3 inches and halved lengthwise
Salt and freshly ground black pepper to taste
¼   cup chopped chives
2   medium shallots, chopped
2   tablespoons unsalted butter
4 to 8 slices truffle, (or 1 to 2 teaspoons truffle oil)

MAKES 4 SERVINGS

Place half the olive oil in a medium-size, heavy skillet and heat until the oil is extremely hot (but be careful not to burn it). Toss the prepared mushrooms into the pan and sauté in the hot oil. Place the remaining olive oil in a second pan over medium heat and add the prepared asparagus. Sauté until tender and remove from the heat. Season the mushrooms with salt and pepper, add the chives and shallots, and toss to combine. Add the butter to the asparagus, and stir until the butter is melted and the asparagus is coated.

To serve: Place the mushrooms in the center of a small plate, top with the asparagus slices, and add 1 or 2 slices of truffle or drizzle lightly with truffle oil. Serve immediately.

Wine Match: This rich, aromatic dish needs to be complemented by an aromatic wine, such as a Pinot Noir. Look for a vintage with plenty of fruit and a crisp strawberry-rhubarb-like acidity. A New Zealand wine from the Marlborough region or a Santa Barbara County vintage is a great choice.

Marinated Squab with Spinach and Tomatoes

This is one of our recipes that needs a little more time to prepare, but much of it can be made in advance. Don't let the number of steps scare you off. Each step is easy — and the end result is worth the effort. At Carlos', we serve this as an appetizer, but it can be used as a light main course. You may need to order your squabs in advance.

MARINADE AND SQUABS:

½ cup olive oil
2 shallots, thinly sliced
3 cloves garlic, peeled and smashed
3 sprigs thyme, leaves only
10 peppercorns
2 sage leaves
1 bay leaf
4 squabs, cut into pieces, about 4 pounds total

CONFIT:

1 cup duck or chicken fat (use more or less, as desired)
2 shallots, minced
2 sage leaves
2 sprigs thyme, leaves only
2 cloves garlic, peeled and smashed
5 peppercorns
1 bay leaf

SQUAB SAUCE:

3 tablespoons olive oil
1 large onion, coarsely chopped
3 stalks celery, coarsely chopped
2 large carrots, sliced in rounds
¼ cup whole coriander seeds
1 quart squab or chicken stock
5 ounces foie gras, cut into small dice

MAKES 4 SERVINGS

To marinate the birds: Combine the olive oil, shallots, garlic, thyme, peppercorns, sage, and bay leaf in a large bowl, and marinate the squab breasts overnight in the mixture. The squab legs will be used in the next step.

To make the confit: Preheat the oven to 375 degrees F. Cover the squab legs with the duck or chicken fat in a small ovenproof dish and place in the preheated oven until the fat has melted. Sprinkle with the shallots, sage, thyme, garlic, peppercorns, and bay leaf. Reduce the oven temperature to 250 degrees F. and cook for 1 to 2 hours, or until the meat starts to release from the bone. Remove from the oven and chill in the melted fat.

To make the squab sauce: Heat the olive oil in a 3-quart pot, and sauté the onion, celery, and carrots just until they begin to brown and soften. Add the coriander seeds and brown lightly. Add the stock and heat until reduced by half. Add the foie gras and stir until melted, about 10 to 15 minutes. Strain again to remove the foie gras solids. Just before serving, warm the sauce and emulsify it with a hand blender.

To prepare the vegetables: Preheat oven to 350 degrees F. Spread a thin layer of olive oil on a small sheet pan. Cut the tomatoes in half and scoop out the soft inside flesh, leaving only the shell of the tomato. Cut the shell with a round cookie cutter to create rounds that are 1 to 1½ inches in diameter. Place the tomato rounds on the oiled pan and turn to coat (see Note). Place a thin slice of garlic on each round, sprinkle with a few thyme leaves, and season with salt and pepper. Place in the oven for approximately 5 minutes, or until just heated through. Remove from oven and keep warm. (This, too, can be done in advance; if so, reheat tomatoes in an additional 1 tablespoon of butter just before serving.)

Wilt the spinach just before serving by melting 2 tablespoons of the butter in a large skillet. Add the spinach in batches and stir until the spinach is coated and wilted. Season to taste with additional salt and pepper.

Olive oil

3   large tomatoes, peeled

2 to 3 cloves garlic, thinly sliced

1   sprig thyme, leaves only

Salt and white pepper to taste

1   pound baby spinach

2½ tablespoons unsalted butter, divided

1   stick of salsify, peeled and julienned into 3-inch pieces

SQUAB PREPARATION:

2   tablespoons Clarified Butter (page 220)

Salt and freshly ground black pepper to taste

1½ teaspoons unsalted butter

Blanch the julienned salsify in boiling water just to soften and then place in an ice bath to stop the cooking. Just before serving, melt the remaining butter in a small skillet just until the butter starts to brown. Add the salsify and heat through, being careful not to burn. Remove from the heat and season to taste with additional salt and pepper.

To prepare the squab: Heat the Clarified Butter in a large skillet (not nonstick) just until it starts to smoke. Season the squab with salt and pepper. Place the squab breasts in the pan skin side down and sauté for about 2 minutes, or until the skin is lightly brown and crisp. Turn the breasts, add the 1½ teaspoons of butter, and sauté until the second side is brown and crisp, about 1 to 2 minutes. Be careful not to burn. (At Carlos', we serve squab rare. You can cook it a bit more, but don't overcook it or it will dry out.)

To serve: Place a small mound of wilted spinach in the center of each of four large dinner plates, and place 1 or 2 tomato rounds on top. Just to the side of the spinach mound, place the confit and a squab breast. Top with a small pile of overlapping salsify. Spoon the sauce around.

Note: The tomatoes do not need to be cut into rounds with a cookie cutter. You can just slice them into wedges. To easily peel a tomato, drop it into rapidly boiling water for less than a minute. Run the hot tomato under cold water and the skin will easily rub off.

Wine Match: At first blush, a red Burgundy or domestic Pinot Noir would seem to be our choice, but with the gaminess of the squab, the richness of the foie gras, and all the spices, we chose a fine American Syrah — a wine with plenty of fruit to enliven this dish and provide a sweet impression as a good contrast.

Foie Gras with Apples, Grapes and Peppercorn Beurre Rouge Sauce

This fabulous appetizer needs to be prepared just before serving. It's the perfect chance for your guests to join you in the kitchen while you prepare this dish. The texture of the foie gras, the sweetness of the grapes, and the spiciness of the peppercorns make this a special way to begin any meal.

SAUCE:

1 teaspoon olive oil
1 teaspoon canola oil
1 shallot, coarsely chopped
1 clove garlic, smashed
6 whole black peppercorns
1 bay leaf
1 cup port wine
1 tablespoon ground black pepper
8 tablespoons (1 stick) unsalted butter, softened, cut into pieces
Pinch of salt

FOIE GRAS AND FRUIT:

1 pound foie gras, cut into 8 slices
Salt and freshly ground black pepper to taste
1½ teaspoons olive oil
1 Fuji apple, peeled and cut into small dice (see Note)
1½ cups red seedless grapes, sliced in half
1 large shallot, minced
1½ teaspoons minced chives

MAKES 4 SERVINGS

To make the sauce: Heat the oils in a heavy medium-size skillet. Add the shallot and garlic, and cook over low heat so they give up some liquid but do not brown. When the vegetables are tender, add the peppercorns and the bay leaf, stir to combine, add the wine and ground pepper, and stir again. Increase the heat and cook for about 5 to 10 minutes, until the sauce has reduced in volume to about 3 tablespoons. (Be careful — the alcohol could ignite while it is burning off; if it does, cover the flame quickly with another pan to extinguish the flame.) Whisk the sauce occasionally.

Remove from the heat and whisk in the butter a piece at a time. (There should be enough residual heat to melt all the butter, but if it cools too much, briefly return to a moderate flame to warm the sauce, and continue melting the remaining butter.) Add the salt and an additional pinch of black pepper. Adjust seasoning to taste. Set aside and keep warm.

To prepare the foie gras: Heat a large, seasoned cast-iron skillet (or a nonstick sauté pan) until it is very hot and is smoking. Liberally season the foie gras on both sides with salt and pepper, and then sear the foie gras, 2 or 3 slices at a time, in the skillet until it is golden. Turn the slices and repeat on the second side. Drain on paper towels and pat to remove excess fat.

Heat the olive oil in another heavy skillet, add the diced apple and the grape halves, and toss to coat and heat through. Add the shallot and chives, and toss again. The apples will brown slightly, but do not burn the shallot.

To serve: Place the apple-grape mixture in a small pile in center of each of four medium dinner plates. Place two slices of foie gras overlapping on top of the fruit, spoon the warm sauce over the foie gras and around the plate, and serve immediately.

Note: Other sweet, crunchy apple varieties, such as Red Delicious or Pink Ladies, can be substituted.

Wine Match: A dish with foie gras is classically paired with a Sauternes, and you'll do fine picking one. Alternatively, choose a wine with a slightly higher acidity, such as an Auslese or Beerenauslese from Germany. Either will provide your palate with a fabulous taste experience.

Tip: This is an example of a recipe where we sauté in a combination of olive and canola oils. We often use a 50/50 combination or some other ratio that we believe will give the dish just the right flavor.

Roasted Vegetable Terrine with Roasted Garlic-Carrot Sauce

pictured on page 70

We serve this terrine as a first course but it would make a fine lunch entrée, too. The terrine is beautiful to look at, incredible to taste, and fun to make. At Carlos', we choose the vegetables for this dish based on color, texture, and taste, but the most important thing is that they're in season. In other words, your choices can be different from ours. This needs to be prepared a day in advance.

SAUCE:

- ¼ cup carrot juice (extract the juice from 2 large carrots or use fresh or frozen carrot juice)
- 1 teaspoon Roasted Garlic Purée (page 222)
- ⅔ cup canola or vegetable oil

Salt and white pepper to taste

VEGETABLE TERRINE:

- 5 plum tomatoes, quartered
- ½ cup Balsamic Vinaigrette (page 210), approximately
- 5 sprigs thyme, leaves only, cut into small pieces
- 2 baking potatoes, peeled and thinly sliced

MAKES 8 TO 10 SERVINGS

To prepare the sauce: Heat the carrot juice and Roasted Garlic Purée until the mixture is warm to the touch. Slowly whisk in the oil with a pinch of salt and pepper until mixture is slightly thickened. Adjust seasoning, strain, and refrigerate the sauce.

To prepare the vegetables: Brush the tomatoes with Balsamic Vinaigrette, place a small sprig of thyme on each, and place in the oven at its lowest temperature for at least 8 hours. The tomatoes will be dry, but they will not be hard, and some moisture will still remain. (If that's impractical for you, here are two alternatives. If your oven has a pilot light, simply place the tomatoes in the oven with the oven off. Or, if your oven does not have a pilot light, substitute the freshest sun-dried tomatoes.)

Now prepare the vegetables. Preheat the oven to 400 degrees F. Brush each slice of the potatoes, squash, watermelon radishes, zucchini, eggplant, asparagus, and mushrooms with Clarified Butter, and sprinkle with salt and pepper. Place the squashes, radish, zucchini, and eggplant on one sheet pan, and place the potatoes on a second sheet pan. Roast until the vegetables have softened — about 3 to 5 minutes for the pan with the squashes, and, if necessary, an additional 2 minutes for the pan with the potatoes. Remove and let cool. Stack each type of vegetable on a plate and refrigerate.

Meanwhile, brush the asparagus with Clarified Butter and broil until al dente. Brush the prepared mushrooms with Clarified Butter and bake as you cook the other vegetables. The mushrooms take about 10 minutes and should be tender when pierced with a sharp knife. Let the mushrooms cool completely, then turn each mushroom on its side and slice into two rounds.

All the vegetables may be prepared the day before and refrigerated in separate stacks.

To assemble: Line a 10- to 12-inch terrine mold (in a half-moon, square, or rectangle shape) with plastic wrap. The wrap should cover the bottom and the inside surfaces and

2   sweet potatoes, peeled and thinly
     sliced
4   purple potatoes, peeled and thinly
     sliced
1   large butternut squash, peeled and
     thinly sliced
2   yellow squash, unpeeled and
     thinly sliced
2   watermelon radishes, thinly sliced
2   zucchini, thinly sliced
1   eggplant, peeled and thinly sliced
10   asparagus spears, grilled
4   Portabello mushrooms, peeled, ribs
     removed, roasted, and sliced
     horizontally
1 to 2 cups Clarified Butter,
     approximately (page 220)
Salt and white pepper to taste

should drape over the outside. Starting at one end of the terrine, drape the eggplant slices up the sides of the mold so that half of the slice is draped over the rim of the terrine. Coat the slices well with Clarified Butter. Layer the other vegetables, one type at a time but saving the mushrooms for last, and coat each layer with Clarified Butter. Top with mushroom rounds. Fold the eggplant slices over the top, brush with Clarified Butter and then seal with the overlapping plastic wrap. Press down to compress the terrine, and puncture the plastic wrap to allow moisture and air to escape. Finally, place some weights over the top of the terrine to continue compression. Refrigerate overnight to set.

To serve: Remove the sauce from the refrigerator and let it come to room temperature. Remove the terrine from the refrigerator, peel back the plastic wrap, and, on a clean, flat surface, invert and remove the metal mold. Carefully peel off the remaining plastic wrap. Cut into slices $1/4$ to $1/2$ inch thick. Place 2 overlapping slices off-center on a large plate. Re-blend the room-temperature carrot-garlic sauce and spoon a pool of the sauce around the slices.

Wine Match: Here we need something light and aromatic, such as a Sancerre from the Loire Valley in France. We also like a new rising star from South Africa: a Chenin Blanc. Both types of wine exhibit a good core of minerality with beautiful floral overtones that match well with a vegetable dish.

**Roasted Vegetable Terrine with
Roasted Garlic-Carrot Sauce
(recipe on page 68)**

Bruschetta with Tomato, Goat Cheese and Basil

This casual presentation can be an appetizer, a passed hors d'oeuvre, or a lunch entrée. It is sure to become one of your favorites. The quantity of the ingredients will depend on how many you want to serve, so vary these amounts if you wish. This dish should be prepared just before serving.

2 to 3 large tomatoes, sliced about ¼ inch thick

Salt and freshly ground black pepper to taste

6 tablespoons Balsamic Vinaigrette (page 210), divided

1 French bread baguette, approximately 20 inches long, halved lengthwise (see Note)

½ cup olive oil

4 ounces goat cheese, crumbled

8 fresh basil leaves, finely chopped

MAKES 4 TO 6 SERVINGS

Sprinkle the tomatoes with salt and pepper, drizzle with 2 tablespoons of the Balsamic Vinaigrette, and broil on both sides for about 15 seconds. Drizzle the cut side of the rolls with the olive oil and then with the remaining vinaigrette, being sure that the full surface of the bread is coated. Sprinkle with additional salt and pepper, and broil to lightly toast. Reduce the broil setting and set the oven temperature to 350 degrees F.

Scatter the crumbled goat cheese over the toasted bread, top each piece with grilled tomato slices, and bake in the oven for about 10 minutes, or until the cheese is softened. Watch carefully to prevent burning. Remove from the oven, sprinkle with the chopped basil leaves, cut into finger-size portions, and serve.

Note: If you prefer, cut the bread into individual rounds, drizzle both sides of the rounds with oil and vinegar, toast both sides, then top one side with tomatoes and cheese, and then bake as above.

Wine Match: Look for a bubbly wine for this dish — but definitely not a Champagne. A good Asti Spumanti or Prosecco from Italy would do the job well. It would provide a lively fruit flavor combined with plenty of palate-cleansing bubbles. Suggested alternative: a glass of cold Lager.

Is there anything more inviting than the aroma of a great pot of soup cooking on the stove? We doubt it. It immediately turns a house into a comfy, cozy home. The aroma of soup has a way of conjuring up images of favorite grandparents or parents and of recipes passed from generation to generation. Soups have a special way of warming our hearts and our stomachs at the same time.

Some of Carlos' soups came to us from relatives and some were created by our talented chefs. But they all have the same basic beginnings — the freshest ingredients. And they're all easy to make. The final seasonings are generally up to the taste of the chef. One might like a bit more salt, another a dash more pepper. Those choices are left to the end, when the flavors of the soup have had a chance to thoroughly combine. Our tip for great soups is to try them often and adjust the flavor to your own taste.

One of the nicest things about making a pot of soup is that very little can go wrong. Most of our recipes can be doubled and frozen for use at a later date. We encourage you to ladle the portions you will use later into strong, plastic freezer containers. Mark the containers clearly with the number of portions and the date. We think that 3 months is the limit for keeping a soup in the freezer. (We never freeze our soups at the restaurant, but you certainly may.) In this chapter, we present an interesting variety of soups. From Cold Cucumber Soup to a classic Vichyssoise, we know that you will create soups that your family and friends will enjoy. Soup's on!

Great salads begin with great ingredients. So many people think that "all salads are equal," but we know that isn't true. Our salads are inventive and delicious — never boring, limp, or tasteless. What differentiates a salad at Carlos' from the "garden variety" is our ability to combine the textures of many different kinds of lettuce with other exciting, crisp, flavorful vegetables. Our dressings are made daily from a combination of the highest-quality oils and full-bodied vinegars. Occasionally, we add some mustard. Then we season the dressing with fresh herbs and spices that produce a beautiful coating for the chosen vegetables.

We suggest that you tear the lettuce with your hands and gently toss the vegetables with the dressing. This can prevent bruising, which can cause a bitter taste. Add the dressing a little at a time, adjusting the amount to your own taste.

For creating a salad, your choices are limitless. Be creative and add other vegetables, fruits, grains, or nuts. Make your salad into a complete meal with the addition of some chicken, fish, or your favorite cut of beef. With some fine bread, you'll have a meal that would please anyone. Truly, the salad has come a long way since its beginning in the "Iceberg Age."

soups and salads

the recipes

COLD CUCUMBER SOUP 77

VICHYSSOISE 78

CHAMPAGNE GINGER-CARROT SOUP 80

CREAMLESS JERUSALEM ARTICHOKE SOUP 81

LEEK AND WINTER SQUASH SOUP WITH GRUYÈRE CROUTON 83

SPRING PEA SOUP 84

FRESH HERB SALAD WITH SWEET PEPPER OILS 85

ASIAN PEAR SALAD WITH CARAMELIZED WALNUTS AND STILTON CHEESE 86

JICAMA-MELON SALAD WITH BELGIAN ENDIVE AND APPLE-BASIL EMULSION 89

SMOKED TROUT SALAD WITH MÂCHE AND TARRAGON DRESSING 90

Cold Cucumber Soup

This is an old standby for a fine French restaurant, yet it seems to make its way to the top of our menu every summer. It makes for a delicious, refreshing way to begin a meal on a hot day.

6   English cucumbers, peeled, seeded, and coarsely chopped

2   cups plain yogurt

1½   cups regular sour cream

1   teaspoon dry mustard

Salt and white pepper to taste

4   large shrimp, tails removed, grilled, and chilled, for garnish

¾   pound lump crabmeat, for garnish

1   large cucumber, peeled and cut into tiny balls, for garnish (see Note)

MAKES 4 SERVINGS

Purée the 6 cucumbers in a blender with the yogurt, sour cream, and dry mustard, and season with salt and pepper. Transfer to a covered container and chill at least 6 hours.

To serve: Slice each of the chilled shrimp almost in half the long way. Place a piece of shrimp in the center of each of four large bowls, place 1 tablespoon of crabmeat and a few small balls of cucumbers next to each shrimp, and ladle a portion of the cold soup over the garnishes.

Note: If you do not have a small melon baller, cut the cucumber into small dice.

Wine Match: The best drink with this soup is chilled vodka, but if you prefer wine, try a rosé.

Vichyssoise

This is a simple recipe for an old French favorite. Although this soup is traditionally served cold, it is also a fine hot soup. To prepare it properly, cook it slowly to bring out the best flavors from the vegetables. Be sure to adjust the seasonings just before serving.

3   tablespoons unsalted butter (or up to 5 tablespoons, to taste)

4   leeks (white part only), trimmed and thinly sliced

1   medium onion, thinly sliced

2   shallots, thinly sliced

12   ounces baking potatoes, peeled and cut into large dice; approximately 2 medium potatoes

6   cups chicken stock

Salt and white pepper to taste (see Note)

1   cup heavy cream

Chives, finely chopped, for garnish

MAKES 6 SERVINGS

Melt the butter in a medium saucepan over low heat. Add the leeks, onion, and shallots, and cook until tender but not browned. (You want to "sweat" the vegetables, not sauté them. You may cover the pot to trap the steam, but you still must be careful not to allow the vegetables to burn.) Add the potatoes and stock, stir to combine, cover the pot, and reduce to a simmer. Cook very slowly, until the potatoes are tender, about 20 to 30 minutes. Season with salt and pepper.

Pour the soup into a large bowl and, using a hand blender, slowly purée it. Strain the soup back into the pot through a fine sieve, pressing down on the solids (there'll still be some stringy solids from the leeks) to extract all of the liquid. Discard any solids, and bring the soup to a boil.

In a separate bowl, whisk the cream with a small amount of the hot soup. Slowly combine the cream and soup, whisking constantly. Taste the soup and adjust seasonings. Refrigerate until cold. Garnish with a sprinkle of chives.

Note: Do not use black pepper or your white soup will be speckled with little black dots.

Wine Match: We like a mid-bodied red wine with this soup. The leeks and cream make us think of a Burgundy with its uncomplicated rusticity. We suggest a Santenay.

Tip: Because leeks are grown in sand, they are very gritty. They are a delicious addition to this soup and other recipes, but they must be cleaned thoroughly. For this soup, cut off the green end, split the white bulb in half, separate the parts, and let cold water rinse through. To be extra sure that your leek is free of any grit, take the cleaning further and place the leek in cold water overnight. Rinse again, then slice into thin pieces. (If you'd like, reserve a few thin leek strips, sauté them in a small amount of oil, and use them as another garnish.)

Champagne Ginger-Carrot Soup

Served hot or cold, depending on the season, this soup is sure to become a favorite. The flavors meld to a rich, creamy taste that makes a hearty start to any meal. The ginger adds a perk to the overall flavor of the soup without overpowering it. You do not need to use a fine Champagne for this recipe, but it couldn't hurt.

¼ cup olive oil

16 tablespoons (2 sticks) unsalted butter, divided

1 medium onion, cut into medium dice

2 shallots, cut into medium dice

4 cloves garlic, minced

2 tablespoons minced fresh ginger

3 stalks celery, cut into medium dice

4 cups carrots, cut into medium dice

1 medium potato, peeled and cut into medium dice

1 tablespoon curry powder

2 cups Brut Champagne

1½ teaspoons Tabasco sauce

4 cups chicken stock

½ cup heavy cream

Salt and white pepper to taste

Chives, finely chopped, optional garnish

MAKES 4 TO 6 SERVINGS

Heat the oil and half the butter in a 4-quart pot. Over medium heat, add the onion, shallots, garlic, ginger, and celery, and cook until transparent, about 2 minutes. Add the carrots, potato, remaining butter, and curry powder, and cook 5 minutes more. Add the Champagne and Tabasco, and reduce the mixture by three-quarters. Add the stock and simmer for 30 minutes.

Purée the soup in batches in a blender. Return to the pot, add the cream, and season with salt and white pepper. Cook over low heat for 15 minutes, whisking frequently. Do not allow the soup to burn. Ladle the soup into serving bowls and sprinkle each serving with chopped chives.

Note: This soup can be served cold. For cold soup, add an extra cup of stock and cool completely in an ice bath, whisking frequently.

Wine Match: Go with the spirit of this soup and choose your favorite Champagne. An aromatic white wine also works well with the ginger flavor, for example, one of the varietals from the Alsace region. A Gewürztraminer, with its rich, lychee-nut flavor combined with such fruits as nectarine and apricot, is a beautiful choice.

Tip: When pureeing a hot liquid, always do it in small batches. (The hotter the liquid, the greater the increase in volume.) We put a batch in a blender, cover it with a light towel to allow steam to escape, and turn on the blender. If you fill the blender container only halfway, there won't be so much soup that it will rise up and hit the towel.

Creamless Jerusalem Artichoke Soup

This thick soup is creamy, even though cream is not one of the ingredients. It's especially delicious for lunch or dinner on a cold winter day and it's perfect for dipping a large slice of thick bread. The lemon zest and thyme give it a fabulous flavor. Although it sounds like it would be good cold, it's best served warm. It can be made up to three days in advance and warmed just before serving.

1 tablespoon canola oil blended with 1 teaspoon olive oil

1 large Spanish or yellow onion, diced

1 medium carrot, diced

1 stalk celery, diced

1 large shallot, coarsely chopped

1 clove garlic, smashed

2 pounds Jerusalem artichokes, peeled and coarsely chopped (see Note)

8 tablespoons (1 stick) unsalted butter (or less, to taste), cut into pieces

1 cup white wine

1 sprig thyme (or more, to taste)

1 bay leaf

10 peppercorns

2 to 3 quarts chicken stock (see Note)

Zest of 2 lemons, minced

Salt and white pepper to taste

Julienne vegetables or duck confit, for garnish

MAKES 8 TO 10 SERVINGS

Heat the oil in a large pot, and cook the onion, carrot, celery, shallot, and garlic over low heat until translucent, about 3 to 5 minutes. Do not brown the vegetables. Add the artichokes and butter, and continue cooking over low heat for 15 minutes. Add the wine and stir to combine.

Make a small bag from a piece of cheesecloth and place the thyme, bay leaf, and peppercorns in the bag. Tie the bag with kitchen string and toss it into the soup. Increase the heat and reduce the liquid by three-quarters. Add enough chicken stock to cover the vegetables by 1 inch. Simmer until the artichokes are fully cooked but not falling apart, about 10 to 15 minutes.

Remove the soup from the heat, add the lemon zest, and let cool for 15 minutes. Remove the cheesecloth and purée the soup in small batches in a blender. Return the soup to the pot and season with salt and pepper. Warm the soup just before serving, stirring frequently. If you wish, thin the soup by adding more stock or thicken it by warming it slowly. Refrigerate if you're not serving immediately.

Ladle the hot soup among warm soup bowls, and garnish with julienned vegetables or duck confit.

Note: Jerusalem artichokes are like potatoes but crispier, and they will cause the soup to thicken as it heats.

Note: If you're using canned chicken stock, use salt-free or the lowest-sodium stock possible. When the soup reduces, any salt content will be intensified. If you would prefer a vegetarian soup, use vegetable stock instead of chicken stock.

Wine Match: Two wines come to mind for this soup. One is a Côtes du Rhône, which has an herbal nose and is rich without being too tannic and has an earthy flavor without being overpowering. Or you could choose a Cabernet Franc from the Loire Valley, which would be softer, fruitier, and rounder.

Tip: When you purée the soup, use a regular blender, not a handheld blender, to reach the proper texture. If the soup is made ahead and reheated, it will pale a little in color, but the taste will be the same. Always adjust seasonings before serving.

Leek and Winter Squash
Soup with Gruyère Crouton

Many people love coming to Carlos' in the winter because it makes them feel so warm and cozy, and that's what we like to hear. We love to use the vegetables so abundant during the winter, and this soup is a particular favorite. The hearty flavors of the squash and leeks complement each other and create an elegant comfort food, and you'll love the Gruyère crouton. This soup is delicious on the day that it is made, but you can make it (and the crouton) a day in advance. In fact, we think it gets even better when the flavors have a chance to meld.

SOUP:

4   tablespoons (½ stick) unsalted butter
1   leek, halved, thoroughly rinsed, and coarsely chopped
2   medium carrots, peeled and coarsely chopped
6   shallots, peeled and coarsely chopped
3   celery stalks, coarsely chopped
2   cloves garlic, whole
2   medium butternut or acorn squash, medium-hard, peeled, halved, seeds removed, and coarsely chopped
1   teaspoon celery seed
1   teaspoon cumin
4   cups chicken stock
Salt and white pepper to taste
1   teaspoon honey
½   cup heavy cream

GRUYÈRE CROUTON:

½   French bread baguette
Olive oil
6   slices Gruyère cheese

MAKES 6 SERVINGS

To make the soup: Melt the butter over medium heat in a large pot and sauté the leeks, carrots, shallots, celery, and garlic until translucent, about 3 to 5 minutes. Add the squash, and stir in the celery seed and cumin. Cover the vegetables with chicken stock, cook until the vegetables are soft, reduce the heat, and simmer for approximately 1 hour. Remove from heat and let cool.

Purée the soup in small batches in a blender, and strain each batch. Return the soup to the pot, season with salt and pepper, and, just before serving, stir in the honey and cream.

To prepare the croutons, use either a toaster oven or a regular oven preheated to 375 degrees F. Cut the baguette into ¼-inch slices, and brush each slice with olive oil on both sides. Place the bread slices on a baking sheet, and place in the oven. Toast on one side, turn the bread slices, and place a slice of cheese, cut to the proper shape, on top of the untoasted side of each slice. Return to the oven until the cheese melts, watching carefully to prevent burning.

To serve: Ladle a portion of hot soup into each of six bowls, and float a crouton in center of each bowl. Serve immediately.

Wine Match: Here is a good example of a soup that works really well with an oaked wine. A Chardonnay works nicely with vegetables, and this soup, because of the natural flavors from the squash, needs a buttery, well-balanced Chardonnay, something with a ripe, round fruit flavor that gives off the aroma of a bit of vanilla and cinnamon. That's what barrels do for wine.

Tip: The Gruyère crouton is the perfect topping for this soup, and it is so easy and versatile that you could make it for many other dishes. Many other soups and salads would be perfect for this scrumptious garnish.

Spring Pea Soup

This soup is delicious served either hot or cold. It takes little time to prepare and is a perfect starter for any meal. Although we prefer to strain the soup, we have made it at home many times, skipping the straining, and never regretted it. Once it is puréed, the texture is relatively thick and very creamy. You can't go wrong either way.

3 tablespoons olive oil

1 large Spanish onion, coarsely chopped

12 cloves garlic (yes, 12 cloves!), peeled and left whole

¼ teaspoon crushed red pepper flakes

½ teaspoon black pepper

1 teaspoon white coriander

1 bay leaf

3 cups water

5 cups frozen baby peas

2 cups whipping cream

Salt to taste

Fresh crabmeat, sautéed in olive oil, optional garnish

Fresh mint, finely chopped, optional garnish

Seedless cucumber; peeled and cut into small dice, optional garnish

MAKES 6 SERVINGS

Place the olive oil in a large pot over medium heat and sauté the onions and garlic cloves in the hot oil until tender and translucent, about 2 minutes. Watch that the vegetables don't turn brown. Add the pepper flakes, black pepper, coriander, and bay leaf, stir to combine, and cook for 1 minute. Increase the heat to high, add the water, and simmer for 20 minutes. Add the peas, cream, and salt, stir to combine, bring to a boil, and cook for 5 more minutes.

Remove the bay leaf and place a small batch of the soup into a blender. Cover the top with a clean towel rather than sealing with the blender cover. Purée, then strain through a fine sieve, and repeat until all the soup has been strained. Adjust salt and pepper.

To serve: If you are using the garnishes, place them in the bottom of each bowl, and ladle some soup in the bowl.

Note: If you serve the soup cold, using less cream and more water will improve the texture.

Wine Match: With this soup, we choose a lighter-style Chianti because of the flavor of the Sangiovese grape. It has a mid-weight fruity quality that we love. Or try a young Tempranillo from Spain, which would perfectly complement the earthiness of the peas. Our wine expert, Marcello Cancelli, remembers his grandmother adding a touch of red wine to her pea soup — and that it was terrific. No one's looking, so see what you think.

Fresh Herb Salad with Sweet Pepper Oils

This is a light, delicious salad. Although the salad itself must be made with fresh ingredients, the sweet pepper oils can be made in advance and easily stored in the refrigerator for a myriad of other uses. For example, on a warm summer day, grill a pounded chicken breast and top it with a small amount of this salad. It makes a refreshing lunch or light summer dinner. Serve with a French roll and a cold bottle of crisp white wine, and you'll have a perfect meal.

2   large red bell peppers
2   large yellow bell peppers
$\frac{1}{2}$ cup oil (canola, olive, or a combination)
Salt and white pepper to taste
$\frac{1}{4}$ cup chopped fresh dill
$\frac{1}{4}$ cup chopped fresh chervil
$\frac{1}{4}$ cup fresh basil, cut into julienne strips
$\frac{1}{4}$ cup chopped fresh tarragon leaves
2   tablespoons olive oil

MAKES 4 LARGE SERVINGS

To make the pepper oils: Process the peppers separately in a juicer. In separate saucepans, heat $\frac{1}{2}$ cup of red pepper juice and $\frac{1}{2}$ cup of yellow pepper juice and cook each over medium heat, stirring occasionally to prevent burning, until the liquid is reduced to a syrup consistency, about 15 to 20 minutes. Slowly whisk $\frac{1}{4}$ cup oil into each hot syrup, season with salt and pepper, and chill. This process will produce about 5 tablespoons of each oil.

To make the salad: Combine the dill, chervil, basil, and tarragon, and toss with the 2 tablespoons of olive oil (use a bit less, if desired). Season with additional salt and pepper, and add about 1 tablespoon of each pepper oil. Toss to combine.

To assemble: Place a 3-inch ring mold on each of four medium plates and fill the ring with salad. Remove the mold and drizzle yellow pepper oil on two sides of the salad and red pepper oil on other two sides.

Wine Match: A full-bodied white wine with loads of aromatics is perfect with this salad. We think it calls for a Viognier, either in the white Côte du Rhône form, as in a blend with Marsanne and Rousanne, or as a dominant varietal from California.

Asian Pear Salad with Caramelized Walnuts and Stilton Cheese

If you like Stilton cheese, you'll love this salad. The tart flavors from the vinaigrette contrasting with the sweet flavor and crunchy texture from the nuts make this a perfect salad choice. The pears with their smooth, cool texture add fine taste to this dish. It has been on our menu in many different forms since we opened our doors.

CRANBERRY VINAIGRETTE:

1   tablespoon salad oil
1   teaspoon red wine vinegar
½   medium shallot, chopped
¼   cup cranberry juice
¼   cup chopped fresh cranberries
Salt and white pepper to taste

CARAMELIZED WALNUTS:

1   teaspoon salt
Pinch of cayenne pepper
Pinch of freshly grated nutmeg
¼   teaspoon sugar
⅛   teaspoon chili powder
⅓   cup shelled walnuts
¼   teaspoon olive oil

SALAD:

3   cups fresh mixed greens, cleaned
Salt and freshly ground black pepper to taste
1   Asian pear (or other firm pear), cored and thinly sliced
4   ounces crumbled Stilton cheese
¼   cup finely chopped fresh rosemary, for garnish (optional)

SERVES 4

To make the dressing: Combine all the vinaigrette ingredients and refrigerate for at least 1 hour (overnight would be fine) to blend.

To make the nuts: Preheat oven to 350 degrees F. Combine the salt, cayenne, nutmeg, sugar, and chili powder. Coat the walnuts with the oil and sprinkle with the spice mixture, making sure the nuts are completely coated. Warm a small ovenproof sauté pan on the stovetop, place the nuts in the warm pan, and, stirring gently, move the nuts constantly, to prevent burning, for about 4 minutes. Place the nuts, still in the pan, in the oven and watch them carefully. The idea is for the sugar to caramelize, not to burn, so about 3 to 4 minutes in the oven should do it. When done, place on a sheet pan to cool.

To serve: Place the mixed greens in a bowl, toss lightly with the dressing, salt, and pepper. Divide the greens among four salad plates. Place 7 or 8 pear slices on and around the salad, and sprinkle some of the crumbled cheese around each salad. Place 7 or 8 walnuts around each salad. If you choose, sprinkle a small amount of chopped fresh rosemary over the top of the salad.

Wine Match: The Stilton cheese is our main wine-matching focus. If you were English, you would have some ruby port with this dish. In America, however, port wine is consumed only at the end of the meal, but we need the abundant fruit of a good Port. The perfect U.S. grape varietal is Zinfandel. One piece of advice, though: if this is the first course or a salad course, prepare a main course that will accompany the same Zinfandel you choose here.

Tip: If you wish, use crumbled goat cheese or feta in place of Stilton.

Tip: For a grand presentation, use a phyllo cup to hold the salad (see photo).

Jicama-Melon Salad with Belgian Endive and Apple-Basil Emulsion

This salad has a distinctive lemony taste and makes for a refreshing spring or summer dish. The basil and lemon oils must be prepared at least a day in advance. Purchase them at specialty food stores if you don't feel like making them.

⅓ cup Basil Oil (page 213)

Zest of 1 large lemon, minced

½ cup canola oil

½ teaspoon sugar

1½ cups apple juice

Salt and white pepper to taste

1 medium jicama, peeled and sliced very thin, then diced

½ cantaloupe, peeled and sliced thin, then diced

4 heads Boston lettuce

1 head red Belgian endive

1 head white Belgian endive

1 to 2 plums, diced

16 chive sprigs, 8 blanched, 8 fresh

MAKES 4 TO 6 SERVINGS

Make the Basil Oil as directed on page 213. You will use ⅓ cup, refrigerated, for this recipe.

To make the lemon oil: Place the lemon zest in a small bowl, add the oil and sugar, and whisk to combine. Refrigerate overnight. Strain the oil through a paper coffee filter (which will be a slow process) and refrigerate until ready for use. Make an apple-basil emulsion by very slowly mixing the basil oil and the apple juice with a hand blender. Season with salt and pepper and refrigerate until ready for use. In a separate bowl, gently combine the jicama, cantaloupe pieces, and a bit of lemon oil.

To assemble the salad: Place 3 pieces of the Boston lettuce in the center of each of four large plates. Drizzle with a little lemon oil, and season with additional salt and pepper. Place a 2- to-3-inch ring mold on top of the lettuce leaves and alternate red and white endive leaves standing vertically, like flower petals, in a circle around the inside of the ring. Fill the ring with the jicama-melon mixture, which will help the endive leaves remain standing. Tie the middle of the endive leaves with a blanched chive or two. Holding the tops of the endive, carefully remove the ring mold. Use another chive to secure if necessary. Mix the apple-basil emulsion and surround the salad with the sauce. Dot the sauce with the diced plums, and place any remaining plums on top of the salad. Stand 2 chive batons in the salad.

Wine Match: Along with the melon taste, we have a dominant citrus element, so we need to stay light and sweet. Drink a nice Riesling from the Mosel Valley in Germany — something at the Kabinett level (the lowest level of sweetness in German wines).

Tip: This is a perfect recipe for using one of our favorite kitchen helpers — squeeze bottles. They're great for storing liquids, such as flavored oils, and for dotting serving plates. In this recipe, the Basil Oil, lemon oil, and the basil-apple emulsion can be refrigerated in squeeze bottles until ready for use.

Tip: For everyday serving at home, concentrate on the two colors of the endive, arranging them in an alternating pattern. Place the lettuce on the bottom and arrange the rest of the salad as you wish.

Smoked Trout Salad with Mâche and Tarragon Dressing

Anything "smoked" has an intense taste, but here the smoking is not overpowering. It adds lots of flavor to the texture of the fish. This is a light and flavorful salad, but it can also be served as an appetizer, first course, or simple summer dinner. Because the fish can be purchased in most grocery stores, delis, or fish markets, it's a quick and easy dish to put together.

¼ cup dried lentils

1 small clove garlic, unpeeled

1 sprig thyme

1 teaspoon black peppercorns

1 bay leaf

Salt to taste

2 sprigs fresh tarragon, leaves only, finely chopped, or 2 teaspoons dried tarragon

6 tablespoons olive oil

3 tablespoons champagne vinegar

2 shallots, peeled and chopped

2 smoked trout fillets, about 8 ounces each, each cut into 4 pieces (see note)

8 ounces mâche leaves, cleaned and trimmed

8 chives, optional garnish

MAKES 4 SERVINGS

Place the lentils in a small saucepan, add water to cover, and add the garlic, thyme, peppercorns, bay leaf, and salt. Cook for 8 to 10 minutes, or until the lentils are just tender. You'll have about 1 cup of cooked lentils. Remove bay leaf, drain, and cool.

To make the dressing: Place the tarragon in a bowl with the olive oil, vinegar, and shallots. Whisk to blend and add additional salt and pepper to taste. Whisk again before serving.

To make the salad: Add a small amount of the dressing to the lentils and stir to coat them. Place about ¼ cup of the dressed lentils in the center of each of four salad plates. Place two pieces of fish so they lean against the sides of the lentils, and top with a pile of the mâche leaves. Spoon some dressing around the salad. If you wish, decorate each salad with a pair of chive batons standing in the lentils and mâche.

Note: In place of the smoked trout fillets, you could use smoked salmon, smoked sable, or whitefish chubs.

Wine Match: We need to contrast the smoked fish with some good acidity in a wine that will also dance well with the tarragon and thyme. This calls for a Riesling from Alsace. The crisp, clean, citrus flavors will contrast well with the earthy, oiliness of the fish.

Tip: For a simpler serving, toss the greens and the lentils with the dressing and arrange the trout fillets around the greens.

ENTRÉES

The centerpiece for every fine meal at Carlos' is the entrée. Each night, our menu offers numerous choices, from the meat, fish, poultry, and vegetarian selections of our daily entrées to the greater number of smaller courses on our dégustation menu.

Most of our patrons plan their dinners around their entrée choices. Although there are no hard-and-fast rules for creating the perfect meal, there are some frequent patterns. For example, diners who want a fish entrée generally complement that selection by choosing a starter of soup or some foie gras. But if a diner is in the mood for beef, a lighter fish appetizer would be a likely starter course. So it goes until the pieces of the meal come together to form a cohesive picture of culinary delight.

We have had many years of practice creating fabulous entrées, so it was hard to choose which ones should be included in this book. We went through hundreds of recipes. Finally, with a little help from our staff and a few loyal patrons, we narrowed it down to the ones you will find in this chapter. Many of them are multifaceted, meaning that we usually give you recipes for the featured item as well as for ideal side dishes. This is how we serve at Carlos', and we want you to be able to re-create that experience in your own home.

These are only suggestions, of course. Mix and match any of the sides or choose one of your own. If you are in a hurry, make only a portion of the recipe. In fact, many recipes have segments that you can prepare ahead. Atop each recipe is a paragraph that makes note of such time-saving possibilities. We always urge, whether in this book or anywhere else, that you read the entire recipe before you begin.

We hope you'll be adventurous and try some foods you might never have tasted before. Venison and rabbit come to mind immediately, and our recipes for those less-common foods are really special and are sure to become favorites. As we create each dish, we think about the melding of flavors and textures. The main attraction will be surrounded with vegetables and some form of starch that will enhance the total dining experience. Together, they look beautiful on the plate and taste even better. First bites are savored and, more often then not, sharing begins. No doubt your entrées will be greeted with the same enthusiastic raves that we've heard so often.

entrées

the recipes

SALMON WITH GRILLED VEGETABLES AND ASPARAGUS SAUCE 96

JOHN DORY WITH CRISPY POTATOES, RISOTTO AND TARRAGON SAUCE 98

CHICKEN BREAST ROULADE WITH VEGETABLES, GOAT CHEESE AND MUSHROOM RISOTTO 101

GRILLED BREAST OF SQUAB WITH MIXED CALIFORNIA GREENS AND SUMMER VEGETABLES 102

ROULADE OF DOVER SOLE 105

LOBSTER SOUFFLÉ WITH LOBSTER-TOMATO SAUCE 106

TUNA WITH CARAMELIZED ONION BROTH AND VEGETABLES 109

CHILEAN SEA BASS WITH VEGETABLE COUSCOUS AND SMOKED-TOMATO COULIS 110

SAUTÉED RED SNAPPER WITH STEWED TOMATOES AND BASIL-VANILLA JUS 113

RAGS OF PASTA WITH LOBSTER, PEAS, CHIVES AND CHANTERELLES 114

SAUTÉED SEA BASS WITH BRUNOISE VEGETABLES AND LIGHT CURRY SAUCE 117

SEARED TUNA WITH ONION RELISH AND PORTABELLO MUSHROOMS 118

STRIPED BASS WITH DICED VEGETABLES AND CARROT SAUCE 119

LAMB GATEAU WITH RATATOUILLE, WILTED SPINACH AND GARLIC PURÉE 120

SAUTÉED DUCK BREAST WITH BABY VEGETABLES IN MUSHROOM BROTH 123

PEPPER-CRUSTED VENISON WITH LETTUCE-CABBAGE CONFIT AND BLACK CURRANT SAUCE 124

HERB-CRUSTED CHICKEN BREAST WITH PASTA, VEGETABLES AND ASPARAGUS SAUCE 127

WRAPPED RABBIT LOIN WITH SPINACH, MORELS AND SUN-DRIED TOMATOES 128

BEEF TENDERLOIN WITH POTATOES, VEGETABLES AND CHOCOLATE WINE SAUCE 131

SQUAB WITH ROOT VEGETABLES AND SHALLOT-SHERRY GASTRIQUE 132

GRILLED STRIP STEAK WITH FAVA BEANS, BABY CARROTS, TOMATOES AND MUSHROOMS 134

CHICKEN BREAST WITH BRAISED BELGIAN ENDIVE 135

Salmon with Grilled Vegetables and Asparagus Sauce

Carlos' offers salmon almost every night. Its color and flavor are so distinctive that we have served this fish in at least 20 incarnations — sometimes hot, sometimes poached cold. This one is a summer favorite. We love this dish so much that we frequently make it for our own backyard cookouts. This recipe is so easy that it's perfect for entertaining. It is written for the outdoor grill, although you could easily cook it under your broiler.

Olive oil spray

1 large baking potato

1 large sprig rosemary, leaves only, chopped

10 sprigs thyme, leaves only, chopped

6 sprigs chives, chopped

½ cup fresh lemon juice

2 cups olive oil, approximately, divided

Salt and white pepper to taste

4 salmon steaks, about 6 ounces each

1 large zucchini, thinly sliced

1 large yellow squash, thinly sliced

16 asparagus stalks, tips cut off and reserved

2 tablespoons finely chopped shallots

MAKES 4 SERVINGS

Spray a grill with the olive oil spray and heat until very hot. Peel and thinly slice the potato, soak the slices in water for 1 hour, then dry thoroughly.

Combine the chopped rosemary, thyme, and chives. Make a marinade by combining all but 1 teaspoon of the mixed herbs and the lemon juice, 1½ cups of the olive oil, salt, and pepper. Place three-quarters of the marinade in a large bowl, place the salmon steaks in the marinade, and refrigerate for 1 hour. Turn the steaks after 30 minutes. Reserve the remaining marinade in the refrigerator.

Grill the potato, zucchini, squash, and asparagus tips (save the spears for the sauce), brushing with the reserved marinade as you grill. The vegetables should blacken slightly as they grill, but they should not burn. Place the grilled vegetables on a sheet pan. If made ahead, cover with plastic wrap after the vegetables are completely cool and store in the refrigerator; warm before serving.

To make the asparagus sauce, purée the asparagus stalks in a blender, and strain to remove any solids. Place the asparagus juice in a deep bowl and, using a hand mixer, slowly add the remaining olive oil, mixing at high speed until well blended. Season with salt and pepper, and set aside.

Remove the salmon from the marinade and grill, skin side down, flipping once. Warm the vegetables, and sprinkle them with the chopped shallots and the reserved fresh herbs. Arrange the vegetables on a serving plate with the salmon steaks on top. Spoon the sauce over the vegetables and the salmon.

Wine Match: We have some smoky elements here, and even though fashion may dictate drinking a Pinot Noir with salmon (and we think a Sonoma Coast would do fine), we would be a bit more daring and try a Malbec from Argentina. This wine has an inherently smoky, dark, brooding flavor — not something big and tannic. You will love its plum-like elements.

Tip: Just about any recipe written for a grill can be adapted for indoor broiling. Just remember this: on a grill, the heat comes from below the food, while under a broiler, the heat comes from above. So "skin side up" on the grill means "skin side down" under the broiler.

John Dory with Crispy Potatoes, Risotto and Tarragon Sauce

The combination of the crisp fish over creamy risotto with a marvelous, rich sauce is what makes this dish so delicious. The textures and flavors seem to meld perfectly. If John Dory is not available, use a different firm white fish, such as grouper or halibut. This recipe is sure to become a real favorite. For the photo, we substituted a potato basket to hold the risotto. We topped it with a large prawn dipped in the sauce.

RISOTTO:

1	small onion, finely chopped
1	tablespoon olive oil
1	cup uncooked arborio rice
½	cup white wine
3	cups chicken stock, warm
3	tablespoons unsalted butter
3	tablespoons Mascarpone cheese
½	cup Oven-Dried Tomatoes (page 223)
4	arugula leaves
1	tablespoon chopped chives
1	shallot, chopped

Salt and freshly ground black pepper to taste

FISH AND TARRAGON SAUCE:

4	fillets John Dory (or other firm white fish), about 6 ounces each
1	large egg, beaten
1	medium potato, peeled, cut into ½-inch squares and very thinly sliced
3	tablespoons oil, approximately
4	tablespoons (½ stick) unsalted butter, in pieces
2	tablespoons chopped fresh tarragon
1	tablespoon capers
1	teaspoon lemon juice
1	teaspoon chopped chives
½	small shallot, peeled and chopped

Salt and freshly ground black pepper to taste

12	kalamata olives, chopped, for garnish

MAKES 4 SERVINGS

To make the risotto: Heat a medium skillet and sauté the onion in the oil until the onion is translucent. Add the rice and toss to coat each grain with oil. Brown the rice a bit and add the wine, stirring constantly until the liquid is almost gone. Add the stock about ¼ cup at a time, stirring constantly and allowing each addition to be absorbed before adding the next. The rice should be fully cooked and creamy. After the rice is cooked, add the butter and cheese, and stir to combine. Add the tomatoes, arugula, chives, shallots, salt, and pepper. While making the risotto, prepare the fish. (If you finish the risotto first, keep it warm until you finish the fish.)

To prepare the fish: Brush one side of each fish fillet with some beaten egg and place about 10 pieces of potato on that side of each piece of fish. Brush a little more egg on the potato to help it adhere. Heat some of the oil in a large nonstick pan until the oil smokes a bit. (Use two pans if necessary to fit all the fish fillets.) Gently place the seasoned fillets in the pan(s), potato side down. Don't check the fish too soon or the potato will fall off. When crispy and browned on the sides, about 1 to 2 minutes, gently turn the fillets and finish the cooking, approximately 2 to 3 minutes more. Remove the fillets, pour off the remaining oil, and use the same pan to make the brown butter sauce.

To make the sauce: Heat the butter until it turns slightly brown. Add the tarragon, capers, lemon juice, chives, shallots, salt, and pepper. Stir to combine.

To serve: Place a medium ring mold in the center of each of four dinner plates and fill the mold with warm risotto. Remove the ring and top the mound with a fish fillet. Drizzle with the butter sauce and garnish with chopped olives.

Wine Match: For this recipe, pair the fish with a Chablis because of the wine's pristine, limestone-driven minerality. You will want to choose a clean Chardonnay flavor. (In France, Chablis is made from chardonnay grapes.) Don't choose an oaky wine as it would overpower the fish. A Chablis vinified in a stainless-steel tank is best (Remember, we're not talking about those big jugs of white wine sold as Chablis in America).

Chicken Breast Roulade with Vegetables, Goat Cheese and Mushroom Risotto

This is a special way to serve chicken. Although it looks fancy, it's really not too difficult to prepare — making it perfect for entertaining. The chicken and filling can be made the day before or early in the day and finished just before serving.

CHICKEN AND FILLING:

6 tablespoons canola oil, divided
1 pound spinach leaves, stemmed
½ pound mushrooms, sliced
1 medium roasted red bell pepper, peeled, seeded, and cut into small dice
1 tablespoon goat cheese
Salt and freshly ground black pepper to taste
6 boneless chicken breast halves, butterflied and pounded thin
Kitchen twine

RISOTTO:

¼ cup canola oil, divided
½ small onion, cut into small dice
1 cup uncooked arborio rice
1 cup white wine
2 to 3 cups chicken stock, warm
1 pound mushrooms, any variety, sliced
3 ounces sun-dried tomatoes, chopped
2 tablespoons chopped chives
2 medium shallots, chopped
2 tablespoons unsalted butter
2 tablespoons heavy cream
Salt and freshly ground black pepper to taste
½ cup grated Parmesan cheese
Red Wine Syrup (page 227), optional

MAKES 6 SERVINGS

To make the chicken filling: Place 2 tablespoons of the oil in a large skillet, heat the skillet until it is very hot, and sauté the spinach leaves until they have wilted. Let the spinach cool slightly, squeeze out the liquid, and place the spinach in a large bowl. Sauté the mushrooms in 2 tablespoons of the remaining oil until they are golden. Add the mushrooms and diced peppers to the spinach in the bowl, stir in the goat cheese, season with salt and pepper, and mix well.

Place a portion of the spinach mixture atop each chicken breast, roll each piece of chicken into a cylinder, and secure the roll with kitchen twine. Refrigerate until you're ready to finish the dish.

To make the risotto: Heat half the oil in a medium skillet over medium heat and sauté the onion until it is translucent. Add the rice and sauté for 3 to 4 minutes until each grain is coated. Add the wine and cook, stirring constantly, until almost no liquid remains. Add the stock about ¼ cup at a time, stirring constantly and allowing each addition to be absorbed before adding the next. Keep adding until the risotto won't take any more liquid. Meanwhile, sauté the mushrooms in a large skillet in the remaining oil for 3 to 5 minutes.

When the rice is almost al dente, add the prepared mushrooms, sun-dried tomatoes, chives, shallots, butter, cream, salt, and pepper, and cook until the liquid is absorbed. Add the cheese, and stir to combine. If the risotto is finished before the chicken, keep it warm until you're ready to serve.

To finish the chicken: Preheat the oven to 425 degrees F. While the oven is heating, sauté the chicken rolls in the remaining oil from preparing the chicken and filling. Cook until the rolls are golden brown on all sides. Roast in the oven for about 8 minutes, or until done.

Remove the twine from the finished chicken, and cut each roll into 1-inch-thick slices. Stir the risotto once more, spoon some onto the center of each of six dinner plates, and fan the chicken slices over the risotto. Drizzle Red Wine Syrup around the plate, if desired. Serve at once.

Wine Match: This dish, with its complex filling, is rich and satisfying. We need a counterbalance, a cleansing wine with refreshing qualities. Quite a few selections qualify, but we recommend a Sauvignon Blanc. Choose a New Zealand wine, for example, for its minerality and grapefruit flavor, or go with a Pouilly-Fumé from France, with its citrus notes, or a South African wine with gooseberry and kiwi flavors. A good California wine might also be welcome with its hay, grass, and lemony edges. Stay away from too much oak influence, as you want something clean and pristine.

Grilled Breast of Squab with Mixed California Greens and Summer Vegetables

This squab is fabulous — tender, juicy, and delicious. If you don't like squab, adapt this recipe for pieces of chicken. And the salad and dressing are a treat, so use them with many other recipes or as a terrific starter to any meal.

6   squab breasts
Vegetable oil
Salt and freshly ground black pepper to
     taste

TRUFFLE DRESSING:

1   tablespoon balsamic vinegar
1   tablespoon sherry vinegar
½   cup vegetable oil
1   teaspoon chopped black truffle
     peelings
Salt and freshly ground black pepper
     to taste
1   teaspoon chopped chives
½   shallot, chopped

SALAD AND VEGETABLES:

1   pound mixed vegetables, blanched
     (we like a combination of baby
     carrots, turnips, asparagus,
     teardrop tomatoes, pearl onions,
     and mushrooms)
1   cup salad greens (see Note)
Salt and freshly ground black pepper
     to taste

MAKES 6 SERVINGS

To prepare the squab: Set a grill on medium heat. Lightly coat the squab with oil to prevent sticking on the grill, and season with salt and pepper. For medium-rare, grill for about 2 minutes on the first side, and then 1 minute on the second side.

For the dressing, salad, vegetables, and serving: Whisk together all the dressing ingredients, and set the dressing aside.

Now blanch each vegetable. The harder vegetables, such as carrots, turnips, and pearl onions, need more time, about 7 to 10 minutes. The softer vegetables, such as asparagus, teardrop tomatoes, and mushrooms, need less time, about 1 to 3 minutes. Although each group should be blanched separately, you can blanch different vegetables within each group together and you can use the same pot and the same water. When the vegetables have been blanched, remove them from the pot and plunge them into cold water to stop the cooking.

Combine the greens and the blanched vegetables in a bowl, lightly season with salt and pepper, and toss lightly with the dressing.

To serve: Slice the squab breasts diagonally and place a portion of the dressed salad in the center of each of six dinner plates. Fan some squab slices over the greens on each plate, and serve.

Note: Choose your favorite greens. At Carlos', we like a mixture of romaine, baby Bibb, radicchio, and arugula.

Wine Match: This dish is a pretty dance of root vegetables and the squab, so go with a light, red wine. Choose a Gamay — but not just a simple Beaujolais. Go for a Grand Cru, like Moulin-a-Vent from any of the producers in France. This wine has the right amount of earthiness and smokiness, combined with a good blueberry core.

Tip: For a fancier presentation, use a potato basket to hold the salad.

Roulade of Dover Sole

There's something fun about a dish that is transformed into a special, intricate presentation when it's sliced. Dover sole is always a treat, and the crayfish mousse filling in this recipe makes it more so. It's a light fish that's enhanced by many sauces, but this preparation is different. The sauce may sound heavier than the traditional meunière or almondine, but it perfectly balances the fish. The Vegetable Medley is easy to prepare and should be considered as an accompaniment to any dish. Instead of the Vegetable Medley, you could simplify the serving by using a single vegetable — broccoli, for example.

LOBSTER-BASIL SAUCE:

1	tablespoon olive oil
¼	cup coarsely chopped fennel
1	shallot, peeled and coarsely chopped
1	clove garlic, peeled and smashed
3	black peppercorns
1	bay leaf
2	cups Lobster Stock (page 226, or available in many supermarkets and gourmet stores)
1	cup heavy cream

Basil leaves (with stems)

Salt and freshly ground black pepper to taste

1½	cups cooked crayfish tails, cooled (see Note)
12	tablespoons (1½ sticks) unsalted butter, slightly softened
1	teaspoon Roasted Garlic Purée (page 222)
½	teaspoon cayenne pepper
¼	cup heavy cream
2	tablespoons Armagnac
½	teaspoon minced fresh tarragon
½	teaspoon minced fresh basil
½	teaspoon minced fresh mint
½	cup cornflake crumbs
½	cup plain bread crumbs

Salt and freshly ground black pepper to taste

8	fresh Dover sole fillets, skin removed, slightly pounded, about 1¼ pounds total
2	tablespoons oil

FOR SERVING:

Vegetable Medley (page 171)

MAKES 4 SERVINGS

To make the sauce: Heat the oil in a medium saucepot and, over medium heat, lightly sauté the fennel, shallot, garlic, peppercorns, and bay leaf until the vegetables are translucent and just beginning to color, about 4 to 5 minutes. The vegetables should be very tender. Add the Lobster Stock, bring the mixture to a simmer, add the cream, and reduce the sauce by three-quarters, until it lightly coats the back of a spoon. Remove from heat, add the basil leaves, and adjust seasoning.

When cool, strain through a fine-mesh sieve and skim off any fat that may rise to surface. Keep warm in a water bath until ready to use, or refrigerate overnight and reheat gently.

Place three-quarters of the crayfish tails, the butter, Roasted Garlic Purée, cayenne, cream, Armagnac, tarragon, basil, mint, cornflake crumbs, bread crumbs, salt, and pepper in the workbowl of a food processor, and pulse to combine thoroughly until smooth. Do not overmix. When the mixture is smooth, add the remaining crayfish tails and pulse briefly, leaving pieces of crayfish noticeable.

Lay the flattened sole fillets so the side from which the skin was removed is facing up. Spread a thin coat of the crayfish mixture over each. Starting with the tail end of the sole, carefully roll each fillet and secure with 2 toothpicks. Cover the rolls and refrigerate until ready for cooking. (These roulades can be prepared early in the day.)

Preheat oven to 400 degrees F. Place the oil in a large, nonstick, ovenproof sauté pan over medium heat on the stovetop. Place the fish roulades vertically standing in the pan, and sauté until lightly browned. Turn the rolls, and place the pan in the oven for 3 minutes. Remove from the oven, place the fish on a cutting board, and, with a sharp slicing knife, cut each roulade into 2 rounds, cutting between the toothpicks. Place the rounds on a lightly buttered pan and place under broiler for about 1 minute, or until lightly browned but still very moist. Remove from the pan, and carefully remove the toothpicks.

To serve: Center a small bed of the Vegetable Medley (or, if you prefer, the single vegetable of your choice) on each of four dinner plates. Place 4 roulade rounds over the vegetables on each plate, and spoon the Lobster-basil sauce all around.

Note: Crayfish are widely available in supermarkets as well as from fishmongers. In supermarkets, they are usually sold pre-cooked and frozen.

Wine Match: The complex flavor of the crayfish and lobster cream dictates a wine with an earthy, tangy flavor. Pair this with a good Chardonnay and stay away from anything with an oaky flavor.

Lobster Soufflé with Lobster-Tomato Sauce

This rich, delicious entrée makes a beautiful presentation. Although your guests may think otherwise, it's relatively simple, and with advance notice, most fish markets will prepare the lobster meat for you. Although you can make Brioche (page 228), you can also buy it or substitute a dense bread such as challah. Lobster Stock (page 226) provides the best taste, but you could use a simpler Fish Fumet (page 227) or bottled clam juice. Some of our patrons have served this as a brunch entrée. What lucky guests!

2 tablespoons white wine
1 cup heavy cream
2 to 3 slices Brioche (page 228 or store-bought), crusts removed and cut into ¼-inch cubes (you could use another dense bread, such as challah, instead)
2 large eggs, lightly beaten
Meat from 1 steamed or boiled lobster, 1 to 1½ pounds, finely chopped
1 tablespoon chopped tarragon
1 shallot, chopped
1 tablespoon chopped chives
Salt and freshly ground black pepper to taste
Nonstick spray

SAUCE:

1 cup Lobster Stock (page 226, or available in many supermarkets and gourmet stores)
2 teaspoons fennel seeds
3 plum tomatoes, coarsely chopped
1 cup heavy cream
White pepper to taste
Chopped green herbs, such as parsley, tarragon, or chives, for garnish

MAKES 6 SERVINGS

Preheat oven to 350 degrees F. Combine the wine and cream, and soak the bread cubes in the mixture for about 10 minutes. Add the eggs, lobster, tarragon, shallots, chives, salt, and pepper, and mix briefly. Pour into six metal or ceramic molds, each with a capacity of about ½ cup and sprayed with oil. Place the molds in a large pan and add enough water to the pan to come about halfway up the molds. Bake in the oven for about 40 minutes, or until the contents of the molds are firm to the touch.

To make the sauce: Heat the lobster stock, fennel seeds, and tomatoes in a small saucepot over medium heat. Heat the cream separately and add it to the stock. Cook until the volume is reduced by about three-quarters and the liquid is thick and sauce-like. Pour the liquid through a fine strainer and add the pepper. The sauce should not need salt because the lobster stock is already somewhat salty. Carefully remove the lobster mixture from the molds and place the contents of one mold on each of six serving plates. Pour an equal amount of sauce over each mold. Garnish with the herbs.

Wine Match: Here's a dish that can accommodate an oak-influenced wine. We suggest a good old California Chardonnay, albeit a balanced one. The creamy texture and vanilla notes of an oaky Chardonnay will enhance this dish.

Tip: Many soups and sauces, such as the sauce for this recipe, call for white pepper. The reason? So you don't have lots of little black dots running through your dish.

Tuna with Caramelized Onion Broth and Vegetables

Tuna has become a favorite at Carlos'. More and more people request it. It's versatile and its firm texture makes it great for some interesting sauces. This recipe uses onions to enhance the flavor of the fish. The sauce can be prepared in advance and heats up easily. Sage gives the sauce a distinctive flavor, but if you are not a fan of sage, leave it out or reduce the amount. Although the vegetables enhance the presentation, mix and match your favorites.

SAUCE:

- 6   tablespoons olive oil
- 1   large Spanish onion, peeled and thinly sliced
- 2   cups water
- 1   clove garlic
- 1   sprig fresh sage, or to taste
- Salt and white pepper to taste

VEGETABLES AND TUNA:

- ¼   cup olive oil, divided
- 4   fingerling or small red potatoes, peeled and sliced ⅛ inch thick
- Salt and white pepper to taste
- 4   tablespoons (½ stick) unsalted butter, divided
- 8   unpeeled baby zucchini, sliced lengthwise, then cut in half (use more if you like zucchini)
- 40   pearl onions (half red, half white), peeled
- 4   pieces center-cut tuna, about 6 ounces each
- 48   grape tomatoes, half red, half yellow (a smaller number of plum or regular tomatoes would be fine)

MAKES 4 SERVINGS

To make the sauce: Heat the olive oil in a large, heavy skillet, add the onion, and sauté over low heat until they turn a caramel color, about 10 to 15 minutes, stirring frequently to prevent burning. When the onions are caramelized, add the water, garlic, and sage, and bring the mixture to a boil over high heat. Boil until reduced by half, about 10 minutes. Strain out the solids and keep the broth warm. Season with salt and pepper.

To prepare the vegetables: Heat half the olive oil in a heavy, medium-size skillet and sauté the potato pieces until they are tender, about 5 minutes. The edges should be only slightly browned. Season with salt and pepper, remove from the heat, add half the butter, stir to melt, and keep warm. Blanch the zucchini pieces just until tender, then plunge them into ice water to stop the cooking. Bring 2 to 3 cups of salted water to a boil in a medium-size pot, add the onions to the boiling water, and cook just until they are tender; about 5 minutes. Drain and place the onions in the ice water with the zucchini. After a few minutes, drain both.

Season both sides of the tuna pieces with additional salt and pepper. Cover the bottom of a large, heavy skillet with the remaining olive oil, and heat the skillet until it is very hot but not so hot that the oil burns. Sear the tuna on both sides, cooking just until the tuna turns light brown.

Warm the potatoes. In a separate pan, warm the onions and zucchini. Add the remaining butter to the warm vegetables, stir to melt, season with salt and pepper, and add the tomatoes just to warm them.

To serve: Place a piece of tuna in the center of each of four serving plates, and surround the tuna with 4 slices of zucchini. Use a portion of the onions and tomatoes, alternating colors, to make a border, and ladle warm sauce over and around the tuna. Serve immediately.

Note: The sauce can be made a day ahead. Refrigerate it and warm it before serving. For a thicker sauce, do not strain. Instead, discard the garlic clove and sage, place the onions and liquid in a blender or in the workbowl of a food processor with a steel blade and process until the sauce reaches the desired thickness.

Wine Match: It would be easy to jump on the Pinot Noir–tuna bandwagon, but we feel that with such savory fare underneath the fish, we should lift it with a full-bodied white wine with heady aromas and refreshing acidity. Alsace Pinot Gris with its pear and yellow plum flavor profile and floral bouquet works well. Riesling from the same region is always a food-friendly choice because of its zingy acidity. One other wine works well here, almost surprisingly: the old reliable and relatively inexpensive Muscadet from the Loire Valley in France.

Chilean Sea Bass and Vegetable Couscous with Smoked-Tomato Coulis

pictured on page 112

In this light preparation, the fish practically melts in your mouth. The vegetables and couscous provide the perfect textures to complement the fish. Despite the number of ingredients and steps in this recipe, nothing here is difficult. If Chilean sea bass is unavailable, use halibut or another firm, white fish.

COATING:

4 tablespoons (½ stick) unsalted butter, melted
¼ cup unseasoned bread crumbs
¼ cup cornflake crumbs
1 clove garlic, peeled and minced
1½ teaspoons finely chopped fresh mint
1½ teaspoons finely chopped fresh basil
½ teaspoon finely chopped fresh tarragon
½ teaspoon finely chopped fresh Italian parsley
Salt and freshly ground black pepper to taste

HERB BUTTER:

1 teaspoon finely chopped fresh parsley
½ teaspoon finely chopped chervil
½ teaspoon finely chopped tarragon
1 clove garlic, minced
8 tablespoons (1 stick) unsalted butter, softened
¼ teaspoon Pernod

SMOKED TOMATO COULIS:

4 vine-ripe tomatoes, yellow or red, skin removed
Olive oil
1 small onion, cut into small dice
1 clove garlic, peeled and minced
1 shallot, peeled and thinly sliced
2 sprigs thyme

MAKES 4 SERVINGS

To make the coating: Combine all the ingredients for the bread crumbs in a mixing bowl. Refrigerate until ready to use.

To prepare the herb butter: Mash the parsley, chervil, tarragon, and garlic into the softened butter. Add the Pernod, stir to combine, and adjust seasoning. Refrigerate until ready to use. This can be prepared 2 days in advance, or you can freeze the herb butter for 1 month.

To prepare the tomato coulis: Place the skinned tomatoes in a smoker and smoke for 30 to 60 minutes, depending on the desired intensity of smoked flavor. (If you do not have a smoker, this recipe is still delicious. Just skip the smoking.) Place enough olive oil in a medium saucepan to just cover the bottom. Heat the oil, and sauté the onion, garlic, and shallot until translucent, about 5 minutes. Add the tomatoes and sauté briefly, about 3 minutes. Add the thyme, bay leaf, salt, and pepper, and stir gently to combine. Add the chicken stock, bring to a simmer, and cook for 1 hour, or until reduced by half. Remove the thyme sprigs and the bay leaf, and purée in a blender, adjusting the consistency by adding more stock to thin or reducing further to thicken. Strain through a fine sieve, and adjust seasonings to taste. Keep warm if you're using immediately, or refrigerate until ready to use and warm thoroughly before serving. You can make this one day in advance.

To prepare the fish: Rinse the fillets and lightly sprinkle with salt and pepper. Refrigerate until ready to use.

To prepare the artichokes: Bring a medium pot half filled with salted water and with a teaspoon or so of lemon juice to a boil. Place the trimmed artichokes in the water and boil for 30 minutes, or until the artichokes are just slightly firm when pierced with a knife. Remove from boiling water and plunge into ice water to stop the cooking. Cut each cooled artichoke in half.

To prepare the beets: Place the beets in another pot half-filled with boiling water. Boil for 20 minutes, or until cooked through but still slightly firm. Plunge the cooked beets into ice water to stop the cooking. When cool, cut into small dice.

Combine the olive and canola oils, and place a third of the oil mixture in a large skillet. Heat the oil, add the artichokes and beets, and toss to warm through. Add the zucchini and squash, and toss to heat through. Transfer the vegetables to a cookie sheet in a single layer. Sauté the mushrooms in the oil remaining in the pan until they are tender and cooked through. Place on the same cookie sheet. Sauté the baby

1 bay leaf
¼ teaspoon salt
¼ teaspoon pepper
¾ cup low-sodium chicken stock

FISH, VEGETABLES, AND COUSCOUS:

4 Chilean sea bass fillets, each about
   6 ounces
Salt and freshly ground black pepper to
   taste
4 baby artichokes, peeled around
   hearts and stems trimmed
Lemon juice
2 baby yellow beets, peeled and
   quartered
3 tablespoons olive oil
3 tablespoons canola oil
1 medium zucchini, cut into small
   dice
1 medium yellow squash, cut into
   small dice
½ cup shiitake mushrooms, stemmed
   and sliced
½ cup baby spinach, stemmed
1 tablespoon unsalted butter
2 cups chicken stock
1 cup couscous (large-grain)
Salt and freshly ground black pepper
   to taste
8 grape tomatoes, halved, optional
   garnish
Fried leeks (page 22), optional garnish
Chopped chives, for garnish

spinach in the butter until the spinach wilts. Place on the same cookie sheet with the other vegetables.

Bring the chicken stock to a boil in a medium saucepan, and reduce heat to a simmer. Add the couscous and stir occasionally until the stock is absorbed but the grains are still firm. Do not allow the grains to stick to the bottom of the pan. When finished, place the couscous into a large bowl to cool a bit. Add the vegetables on the cookie sheet to the warm couscous, and stir to combine.

To cook the fish: Preheat oven to 450 degrees F. Heat a large nonstick, oven-proof sauté pan, add the remaining oil combination to the pan, and heat until the oil is very hot. When the oil just begins to smoke, add the fish to pan. Sear the fillets on their flesh side until they are golden, then carefully turn the fish over and press a light layer of the prepared coating on the fillets. Place in the oven for 5 minutes (or more, depending on the thickness of the fish). Test for doneness (a toothpick should slide in easily). When the fish is ready, quickly brown the coating under the broiler. Watch to prevent burning. (If the fish is very thin, there is no need to place in the oven for warming; quickly place under the broiler to brown the crumbs.)

To serve: Reheat the vegetables and couscous, and toss with a small amount of herb butter. Add salt and pepper and additional seasoned butter to taste. Mound the couscous in the center of each of four dinner plates (or use a ring mold, if desired). Surround the couscous with the grape tomatoes. Place the fish fillets on top of the couscous, and spoon some warmed tomato coulis around. Garnish with Fried Leeks and lightly sprinkle with chopped chives.

Wine Match: We envision this dish being served outdoors on a beautiful summer day with your guests sipping on a Puligny-Montrachet. This white Burgundy works beautifully. Choose any white wine with mineral notes, such as an Italian Sauvignon Blanc.

Tip: To skin tomatoes, rinse them and cut a shallow X in the bottom of each. Place them in boiling water for 1 minute, until the skin releases. Plunge them into ice water to stop the cooking, then remove the skin, which should slip off easily.

Tip: Eliminate the garnishes if you'd prefer a simpler presentation at home. And you could simply spoon the couscous onto the plates without using a ring mold.

Chilean Sea Bass and Vegetable Couscous with Smoked-Tomato Coulis (recipe on page 110)

Sautéed Red Snapper with Stewed Tomatoes and Basil-Vanilla Sauce

This easy preparation is delicious for lunch or a light summer supper. If you don't like snapper, substitute another firm white fish. The combination of the different varieties of tomato really makes the flavors blend to excite the palate. It used to be that these varieties were available only at certain times of the year, but now you can find most of them during any season. If one is not available, substitute another.

BASIL-VANILLA SAUCE:

6   medium-size basil leaves
2   vanilla beans, cut in half, slit lengthwise, insides scraped out and reserved
Pinch of coarse salt
Pinch of white pepper
1½ cups water

VEGETABLES:

1   tablespoon olive oil
1   large tomato, quartered
16   teardrop yellow tomatoes, 8 halved, 8 whole
28   red currant tomatoes or 14 grape tomatoes
4   cherry tomatoes, cored and halved
2   plum tomatoes, cored and quartered
1   sprig thyme, leaves only
Salt and white pepper to taste
3   sage leaves, chopped
1   tablespoon unsalted butter

FISH:

4   red snapper fillets, each about 8 ounces
Salt and white pepper to taste
Olive oil
4   tablespoons (½ stick) unsalted butter

MAKES 4 SERVINGS

To make the Basil-Vanilla Sauce: Place the basil leaves in a small saucepot. Add the scrapings from the vanilla beans and the beans themselves to the basil, along with the salt, pepper, and water. Boil over high heat for about 10 minutes, or until the mixture is reduced by half. Remove from the heat and keep warm.

To prepare the vegetables: Preheat oven to 400 degrees F. Pour the olive oil in a large, heavy, ovenproof skillet. Cut out the centers of the tomato quarters, leaving only the meat on the skin. Slice each piece into thin strips. Place all the tomatoes in the skillet, add the thyme, salt, pepper, sage, and butter, and cook over high heat just until vegetables start to boil. Place the skillet in the oven and cook for 5 more minutes. Keep the oven on.

To cook the fish: Season the fish fillets on both sides with salt and pepper. Using a very sharp knife, turn the fillets skin side up and make several shallow, diagonal slits in the fish. Rotate the fish and repeat, forming a diamond pattern on the skin. Lightly coat the bottom of a large ovenproof skillet with the olive oil, and heat the skillet on the stovetop just until it smokes. Place the fish in the skillet, skin side down, and shake the pan to prevent the fish from sticking. Cook until the skin is golden brown. Turn the fish skin side up, dot with the butter, and place in the oven for 6 minutes or until cooked to desired doneness. (At Carlos', we serve the fish medium-rare).

To serve: Spoon some of the tomato mixture into the middle of each of four large, shallow dinner bowls. Ladle a portion of the sauce, directly from the pot, around the tomatoes. (Don't be concerned about the little black dots. Those are the vanilla beans and they add a wonderful taste.) Lightly pat the fish fillets with a paper towel to remove excess oil and butter, and place a fillet on top of tomatoes. Serve immediately.

Wine Match: This dish has a clear Mediterranean influence, making it great with a Mediterranean wine, such as a Fino Sherry, or with a Sicilian Chardonnay, a full-bodied wine with vanilla overtones that would clearly agree with the sauce. You could also choose a Riesling, Pinot Gris, or Sauvignon Blanc.

Tip: For a hardier variation, add 2 cups of baby spinach to the tomatoes and cook just until the spinach wilts.

Tip: The tomatoes and fish can be cooked entirely on the stovetop. At Carlos', we finish cooking in the oven to speed up the process, so allow a few more minutes for the stovetop method.

Tip: To simplify this dish for home use, replace the preparation of the Basil-Vanilla sauce by buying a prepared pesto sauce and spooning it lightly around the tomatoes.

Rags of Pasta with Lobster, Peas, Chives and Chanterelles

This pasta is one of our favorites, cut into "rags," but it can be used in other shapes to complement many of your favorite dishes. Why are they called rags? Because after they're cooked, they look kind of like rags. We customarily serve this dish warm, but it also works as a cold entrée on a hot, summer day. No time to make your own pasta? Buy some packaged wide noodles or another hearty noodle.

1/3 cup semolina flour

1 cup all-purpose flour, plus additional for dusting

1½ teaspoons salt

1½ teaspoons lemon zest

2 tablespoons chopped and blanched chives

1 large egg

6 tablespoons olive oil, divided

½ cup water, approximately

1 cup peas (fresh or frozen)

4 lobsters, each about 1 pound, cooked and meat removed from shell (see Note)

1 pound chanterelle mushrooms, trimmed

Salt and freshly ground black pepper to taste

2 tablespoons minced chives

4 tablespoons (½ stick) unsalted butter, melted

MAKES 4 SERVINGS

Combine the flours, the 1½ teaspoons of salt, zest, and the chives in the workbowl of a food processor fitted with a steel blade. Add the egg and 2 tablespoons of the oil, and pulse to combine. Add small amounts of the water, just until a semi-moist ball forms when pulsed. Place the dough on a floured surface and knead for 5 minutes, or until it is smooth and elastic. Wrap in plastic wrap and refrigerate at least 1 hour.

Divide the dough into 4 pieces. Set your pasta machine to its widest setting. Feed each piece of dough through the rollers, fold the dough in half, and feed through 5 more times, turning the dough 90 degrees each time. Keep the rest of the dough wrapped until you feed it through the machine. Adjust the machine to the next setting (slightly narrower), and feed the dough through once. Repeat to the next-to-last setting. Flour both sides of pressed pasta and loosely fold up width-wise. Cut into pieces approximately 1½ inches wide. Unfold individual rags and place on a heavily floured pan. Keep covered, so rags will not dry out.

Bring a small pot of salted water to a boil over high heat and cook the peas (either by boiling or steaming) for about 4 minutes, until they are just tender. Drain and set aside to cool.

Place 2 tablespoons of the remaining olive oil in a small pan, and reheat the lobster meat with the peas over low heat. In a separate pan, sauté the mushrooms in the remaining olive oil for about 3 to 4 minutes. Season with additional salt and pepper.

Drop the fresh pasta into a large pot of rapidly boiling water. When the rags float (after about 2 minutes), remove them from the water with tongs and toss with the lobster-peas mixture. Place in the center of each of four serving plates. Add the minced chives to the mushrooms, stir quickly to mix, and top the pasta with equal portions of the mushroom mixture. Drizzle with melted butter and serve immediately.

Note: Instead of buying cooked lobster meat, you could cook the lobsters yourself by plunging them into a stockpot filled with boiling water and cooking for 5 to 6 minutes.

Wine Match: What is it about shellfish and butter that feels so right and tastes so decadently sensual? Here we tone it down a bit with good pasta and savory peas to make it a homey meal. Enhance the dish by serving Champagne (and French Champagne is the one and only), especially a Blanc de Blancs, which is 100 percent Chardonnay. Or go the more affordable route with a Pouilly-Fuissé or a Sonoma Coast Chardonnay. Don't forget that you need some acidity to contrast the earthy mushrooms and all that sensuous, buttery lobster.

Tip: This recipe can be simplified by buying sheets of fresh pasta or boxed lasagna sheets. One-half pound of dried pasta would be the equivalent of about 1 pound of fresh pasta.

Sautéed Sea Bass with Brunoise of Vegetables and Curry Sauce

"Brunoise" means very small dice — about $1/8$ inch in each dimension, and this technique makes the presentation of this special dish especially pretty. Any other white, firm meaty fish may be substituted for the bass.

CURRY SAUCE:

2	tablespoons lime juice
1	clove garlic, minced
1	cup Fish Fumet (page 227) or clam juice (see Note)
1	kafir leaf or bay leaf (kafir available at Asian specialty markets)
1	teaspoon curry powder
$1/4$	cup heavy cream

Salt and white pepper to taste

VEGETABLES:

Olive oil

1	ear of corn, kernels removed
2	red bell peppers, trimmed and cut into small dice
2	yellow bell peppers, trimmed and cut into small dice
2	small zucchini, trimmed, skin on, and cut into small dice
2	small yellow squash, trimmed, skin on, and cut into small dice

Coarse salt and white pepper to taste

FISH:

4	sea bass fillets, about 6 ounces each

Coarse salt and white pepper to taste
Olive oil

4	tablespoons ($1/2$ stick) unsalted butter

MAKES 4 SERVINGS

To make the curry sauce: Combine the lime juice, garlic, Fish Fumet, and kafir or bay leaf in a saucepot. Bring to a boil over high heat, add the curry powder and cream, reduce the heat to medium, and simmer until the mixture is reduced by half. Season with salt and pepper, and keep warm. (If you used clam juice instead of Fish Fumet, be sure to taste for seasoning before adding any more; clam juice is naturally salty.) Remove kafir or bay leaf before using.

To cook the vegetables: Coat the bottom of a large skillet with a thin layer of olive oil. Heat the oil, and sauté the corn until it just begins to soften. Add the peppers and cook with the corn until the dice just begins to soften, then add the zucchini and squash. Toss the vegetables to combine and cook until they are just cooked through but not until they are very soft and falling apart. Season with salt and pepper and keep warm.

To cook the fish: Season the fillets on both sides with salt and pepper. Coat a large skillet with olive oil and heat the oil over high heat until it just begins to smoke. Place the seasoned fish skin side down and cook for about 2 minutes, or until the skin is crisp. Shake the pan to keep the fish from sticking to the bottom. Carefully turn the fillet and cook for about 2 minutes on the second side, or until the fish is cooked to the desired doneness. Be careful not to overcook it or it will be dried out. When done, dot each fillet with 1 tablespoon (or less) of butter.

To serve: Place some vegetables in the center of each of four dinner plates, top the vegetables with a fish fillet, and ladle some sauce all around.

Note: If you use clam juice, keep in mind that its salt content can vary widely. A low-sodium or unsalted liquid is best, but whatever you use, be aware that it will affect the saltiness of the sauce.

Note: Stand the ear of corn on one end, and scrape off the kernels using a sharp knife (see page 93).

Wine Match: The zucchini and bell peppers with the curry seasoning call for a Riesling or Sauvignon Blanc from the Loire Valley. We recommend a Pouilly-Fumé. But if you're a bit more adventurous, look for a Savennieres. This is a Chenin Blanc with lots of mineral characteristics. It has a mouth-filling viscosity that should help clear your palate after each delicious, curried bite.

Tip: There's no question that brunoise — vegetable dice about $1/8$ inch in each dimension — is labor-intensive. We think it makes an especially beautiful presentation, but larger dice would be easier for home serving and would not affect the taste of this dish. Remember, the cooking time would be a bit longer for larger dice.

Seared Tuna with Onion Relish and Portabello Mushrooms

This is a quick and easy recipe. The onion relish can be prepared a day in advance, and, if there are too many peppers for your taste, cut down the quantity. Although we prefer tuna seared on the outside and rare inside, some of our customers request their tuna "cooked through." That's fine, but don't let the tuna dry out.

ONION RELISH:

1	cup red wine vinegar
½	cup water
1½	cloves garlic, peeled and minced
1	whole red onion, peeled and finely chopped
2	teaspoons salt
¼	teaspoon white pepper
5	tablespoons sugar
1	teaspoon chopped thyme leaves
¼	cup olive oil
2	yellow bell peppers, coarsely chopped
2	red bell peppers, coarsely chopped

PORTABELLO MUSHROOM:

1	large Portabello mushroom
½	cup Balsamic Vinaigrette (page 210)

FOR TUNA AND SERVING:

4	tuna fillets, about 6 ounces each

Salt and white pepper to taste
Sweet Pepper Oil (page 214)

MAKES 4 SERVINGS

To make the onion relish: Combine the vinegar, water, garlic, and onion in a medium mixing bowl. Add the salt, pepper, and sugar and mix again. Add the thyme leaves, oil, and peppers, and mix again. Cover the bowl and refrigerate. Warm before serving.

To prepare the Portabello mushroom: Peel off the top layer of the mushroom and gently remove the ribs underneath. The mushroom should basically be white, but don't be concerned if there is a little brown left. Marinate the mushroom in the Balsamic Vinaigrette for at least 1 hour, or overnight, in the refrigerator. Remove the mushroom from the marinade, and broil it for about 3 minutes on each side. Cut the mushroom into thin slices. Reheat before serving.

To cook the tuna: Lightly season the fillets with salt and pepper on both sides. Sear the fish on both sides. The center should be served rare. Cut into thick slices.

To serve: Spoon a portion of onion relish in the center of each of four dinner plates. Top with a portion of tuna slices. Surround with Sweet Pepper Oil. Top with a few slices of grilled mushrooms.

Wine Match: With this dish, pick an Oregon Pinot Noir with its mushroom flavor and earthy notes to complement the Portabello. It also works well with the oil of the tuna. These ingredients marry beautifully with the wine's softer tannins and the red currant and raspberry notes. Stay away from a heavier red wine with fish.

Tip: This recipe would be excellent served with Fresh Herb Salad (page 85). Place the tuna on one side of the plate, the salad on the other. One change, though: Do not drizzle sweet pepper oil to the sides of the salad because you've already done that around the fish.

Striped Bass with Diced Vegetables and Carrot Sauce

This recipe works well with many types of fish. Try it with black bass, Chilean sea bass, snapper, or grouper. We like a certain meticulous vegetable presentation that we believe makes this dish extra special. This confetti of vegetables, with its multitude of colors, creates a celebration on the plate.

3   large carrots, peeled and juiced (or 6 tablespoons carrot juice)
½   cup olive oil, divided
Salt and freshly ground black pepper to taste
1   zucchini, thinly sliced, then diced
1   small yellow squash, thinly sliced and cut into small dice
1   medium red bell pepper, thinly sliced and cut into small dice
1   medium yellow bell pepper, thinly sliced and cut into small dice
1   small eggplant, thinly sliced and cut into small dice
3   shallots, chopped
2   plum tomatoes, diced
4   striped bass fillets, about 6 ounces each, skin on
2   tablespoons unsalted butter, cut into pieces
2   tablespoons chopped chervil or curly parsley, optional garnish

MAKES 4 SERVINGS

Preheat oven to 350 degrees F. Place the carrot juice in a blender, slowly add half the olive oil, blend thoroughly, and season with salt and pepper. Keep warm.

Heat 2 large skillets until they are very hot. Place 2 tablespoons of the remaining olive oil in one skillet and add the zucchini, diced squash, peppers, and eggplant. Stir constantly over high heat until the vegetables are soft, about 2 to 3 minutes. Add the chopped shallots and diced tomatoes, and continue cooking until the shallots and tomatoes are cooked through, another 2 to 3 minutes. If you wish, prepare the vegetables ahead and reheat them before serving.

Season the fish fillets on both sides with additional salt and pepper. Add the remaining 2 tablespoons of olive oil to the second skillet. When the pan is very hot, add the fillets, skin side down, and cook over high heat for 2 minutes, making sure the fish doesn't stick to the pan. The sides of fish should be slightly browned and the flesh should not be translucent. Place the fish pan in the oven for about 4 minutes. Remove the pan from the oven, place it on a low flame, turn the fillets over, dot the fillets with the butter, and cook until the butter has melted, about 1 to 2 minutes.

To serve: Arrange some vegetables in the center of each of four serving plates, reserving a small amount for garnish. Surround the vegetables with carrot sauce. Place a fish fillet on top of the vegetables, skin side up. Place the reserved vegetables on top of fish. Sprinkle with chopped chervil, if desired, and serve at once.

Wine Match: This dish acts as a canvas on which you can display several different shades. Chardonnay agrees with the vegetables and dances with the fish. Try a Côtes Chalonnaise, such as Pouilly Fuissé or St. Veran or maybe even a Macon. You might also try a Sauvignon Blanc, although we advise staying away from the very lean examples. Select a South African wine for its distinctiveness or stick to a Sancerre from France for its traditional reliability.

Tip: At Carlos', we slice the vegetables very thin using a mandoline. For home preparation, you need not be so finely tuned. Just slice and dice the vegetables and you will have a memorable dish.

Lamb Gateau with Ratatouille, Wilted Spinach and Garlic Purée

Although it seems like there are a lot of steps for this recipe, each is relatively simple. The elegant presentation of this dish is exceeded only by its extraordinary flavor, and the ratatouille is great by itself or tossed with your favorite pasta.

RATATOUILLE:

¼	cup olive oil
1	medium onion, peeled and diced
3 to 4 cloves garlic, peeled and minced
½	red bell pepper, diced
½	cup diced eggplant
1	small tomato, diced
1	small zucchini, diced
1	teaspoon finely chopped rosemary leaves
1	teaspoon finely chopped thyme leaves

Salt and white pepper to taste

SPINACH:

1	tablespoon unsalted butter
1	pound fresh baby spinach, stems removed

Salt and white pepper to taste

GARLIC PURÉE:

4	cloves peeled garlic, boiled about 5 minutes until fork-tender
1	tablespoon olive oil
2	tablespoons brandy
2	tablespoons Port wine
4	cups Lamb Stock (page 225)

Salt and white pepper to taste

LAMB:

4	pieces lamb loin, each about 4 ounces and 1 inch thick, not rolled

Salt and white pepper to taste

2	tablespoons olive oil

MAKES 4 SERVINGS

To prepare the ratatouille: Heat the olive oil over medium heat in a medium saucepan, add the onion and garlic, and cook until translucent. Add the peppers and cook until soft, about 3 minutes. Add the eggplant and cook for 3 minutes. Add the tomato, zucchini, rosemary, and thyme, and cook all for an additional 5 to 10 minutes, or until the vegetables are cooked through with most of the liquid cooked off. Season with salt and pepper.

To prepare the spinach: Heat the butter in a large saucepan, and wilt the spinach in the hot butter in small batches by folding over in the pan as each batch of spinach wilts. Season with salt and pepper. Do not overcook. Set aside.

To prepare the garlic purée: Brown the softened garlic in the olive oil in a small pan, being careful not to burn it. Smash the browned garlic with the side of a wide knife. Add the brandy and Port, and cook the mixture until it reduces to form a thick syrup. Reserve the liquid, allow it to cool, pass it through fine sieve, and set it aside. In a large pot, reduce the Lamb Stock by half, add the garlic purée, and season with salt and pepper.

To prepare the lamb: Preheat oven to 475 degrees F. Season the meat on both sides with salt and pepper. Heat the oil in a large ovenproof skillet until it is very hot, and sear the lamb on both sides in the hot oil, then place the skillet in the oven for 3 minutes for rare, or longer to taste. Let the lamb rest for 5 minutes before slicing diagonally.

To serve: Reheat all the vegetables and the sauce. Place a layer of spinach on the bottom of a 3-inch ring mold on a large plate, add a portion of the ratatouille, remove the mold, and fan the sliced lamb on top of vegetables. Surround the lamb with reduced stock and top with a few extra spoonfuls. (If you don't have a ring mold, just layer as described on the plate.) Serve immediately.

Note: We recommend lamb stock, but one of our testers used a store-bought vegetable stock and loved how it turned out.

Wine Match: Although this is a Mediterranean-inspired dish, we prefer an Atlantic-inspired wine, and we can't think of a better match than a good red Bordeaux. Peppers, and lamb washed down with a Médoc wine would be great. The combination of Cabernet Sauvignon, Merlot, and especially Cabernet Franc, directly complement this dish while providing good fruit flavors to counter all its earthiness. Look for a Cru Bourgeois or even a Bordeaux Supérieur, whose wines have vastly improved in recent years. For a special occasion, enjoy a mature Cru Classé.

Sautéed Duck Breast with Baby Vegetables in Mushroom Broth

This dish, which is served like a soup, makes a delicious lunch or dinner selection. It's a favorite in France and we like to think that it's a favorite in our restaurant as well. For variety, this recipe works just as well with chicken or squab breasts.

VEGETABLES:

4 baby artichokes
1 tablespoon olive oil
Juice of ½ medium lemon
12 whole cloves garlic
8 shallots
20 pearl onions

DUCK:

4 duck breasts, each about 6 ounces, bones removed, skin on
Coarse salt and white pepper to taste
Olive oil

MUSHROOM BROTH:

1 clove garlic, crushed or smashed
1 sprig thyme
1½ cups mixed wild mushrooms (chanterelle, Portabello, oyster) or ¾ cup dried mushrooms (see Note)
1 tablespoon porcini powder (do not use if using dried mushrooms — see Note)
Pinch each of coarse salt and white pepper
2 cups water

FOR SERVING:

1 tablespoon unsalted butter
Salt and freshly ground black pepper to taste
2 cherry tomatoes, quartered
8 arugula leaves, stems removed

MAKES 4 SERVINGS

To prepare and cook each artichoke: Remove ½ inch from the base of the stem. Remove the outer leaves and small leaves at the base of the stem. Lay the artichoke on its side and trim ½ inch from the top. Remove any thorny tips or dark green leaves. Cut in half from top to bottom, remove any fine hairs with a small spoon. Remove any dark green areas that you see. Fill a small saucepan halfway with water, add the olive oil and lemon juice, make sure the hearts are floating in the water, then bring to a boil and cook until fork-tender, about 10 to 12 minutes. Remove from the heat and let the artichokes stand in the water. Do not drain them.

To prepare the remaining vegetables: Blanch the garlic cloves in salted water in a small saucepan until fork-tender, about 5 minutes. Watch to make sure they don't get too soft. In another small pot, blanch the shallots and onions in salted water until fork-tender, about 7 to 10 minutes. Drain and reserve.

To prepare the duck breasts: First, render the fat by placing the duck breasts skin side up and making shallow cuts through the meat on a diagonal. Turn the breasts and repeat so that the skin and meat are scored with a diamond pattern. Season all surfaces with salt and pepper. Heat a large skillet and add just enough olive oil to cover the bottom of the pan. When the oil is smoking, place the duck pieces in skin side down. After about 5 minutes, when the skin is crispy and brown, turn the duck and cook on the second side until the meat is done as desired. Let the finished breasts rest about 2 minutes, turning over 2 or 3 times to distribute the juices. With a sharp knife, slice the duck breast on the diagonal.

To make the mushroom broth: Place the garlic, thyme, mushrooms, porcini powder, salt, pepper, and water in a saucepan. Bring to a boil over high heat, simmer for 10 to 12 minutes, remove from the heat, and strain. Adjust seasoning. Set aside and keep warm.

To serve: Reheat the vegetables together on low heat with the butter in a medium skillet. Warm through and season with salt and pepper. Add the cherry tomatoes and arugula just before serving. The arugula will wilt almost immediately. Heat four large, wide bowls. Place a portion of the vegetables in the center of each bowl and spoon the broth around. There should be enough broth to come halfway up the mound of vegetables. Do not cover the vegetables. Fan slices of duck over the vegetables.

Note: If you use dried mushrooms, reconstitute them first according to package directions, and add the soaking water to the broth in place of a like amount of the water you would use to make the broth if you were using fresh mushrooms. Porcini powder can be purchased in Italian delis or specialty markets.

Wine Match: An acidity fruit-laden Pinot Noir with its earthy flavors agrees with the mushrooms yet contrasts the complexity of the duck.

Pepper-Crusted Venison with Lettuce-Cabbage Confit and Black Currant Sauce

pictured on page 126

If you've never tasted venison before, make this recipe your first experience. The sweet flavors of the sauce meld beautifully with the gaminess of the meat, and the cabbage makes a perfect bed for the dish. If you're still not sure about venison, you could make this recipe with beef tenderloin or lamb. This recipe must be prepared a day in advance, so it's perfect for entertaining and spending more time with your guests.

LETTUCE-CABBAGE CONFIT:

¼	cup duck or chicken fat
1	star anise
5	juniper berries
4	cups shredded red cabbage
2	cups Roasted Vegetable Stock (page 224)
1	head Bibb lettuce, washed and left whole

VENISON, MARINADE, AND CRUST:

2	pounds venison loin
1	cup olive oil
2	cups red wine
10	juniper berries
3	star anise
4	cloves garlic, peeled and smashed
1	carrot, coarsely chopped
½	medium yellow onion, coarsely chopped
5	sprigs thyme
1	tablespoon black peppercorns
½	cup coriander seeds, ground medium
2	tablespoons freshly ground black pepper

MAKES 4 SERVINGS

To prepare the confit: Melt the fat with the star anise and juniper berries in a medium pot over a low heat. Add the shredded cabbage and cook for about 10 minutes, until the cabbage has wilted but still has some body. Remove the pot from the heat, remove and discard the star anise and juniper berries, and refrigerate the melted fat and cabbage. Place the Vegetable Stock and the head of Bibb lettuce in a medium pot and cook, uncovered, over medium-low heat until tender, about 20 minutes. Remove, drain, and cool the lettuce. Remove any browned outer leaves, return the lettuce to the stock, and refrigerate. This can all be done a day in advance.

To prepare the venison, marinade, and crust: Place the venison in a glass pan or heavy plastic bag. Combine the olive oil, wine, juniper berries, star anise, garlic, carrot, onion, thyme, and peppercorns in a mixing bowl, and pour the mixture over the venison. Marinate in the refrigerator for at least 24 hours. Turn occasionally. (The meat can marinate for as long as 48 hours.) For the crust, combine the coriander and ground pepper, and set aside.

To make the Black Currant Sauce: Combine the black currant preserves and vinegar in a small saucepan, and cook over low heat, watching carefully to prevent burning, until the volume is reduced by half. Set aside. Brown the venison trimmings in the olive oil in a 3-quart saucepan. (If a crust forms on the bottom of the pot, deglaze with a touch of vinegar to loosen the bits.) Add the coriander, peppercorns, bay leaves, carrots, celery, and onion, and sauté until lightly brown, about 3 to 5 minutes. When thoroughly sautéed, add the stock and the currant reduction, bring to a boil, reduce the heat, and simmer to reduce by half. Add the cream and butter, stir to blend, and keep warm until ready to use or store in the refrigerator. Strain through a fine sieve before serving.

Just before serving: Place 1 tablespoon of the olive oil in a small sauté pan, add the prepared cabbage, shallot, and chives, and warm through. Season with salt and

BLACK CURRANT SAUCE:

¼   cup black currant preserves
¼   cup red wine vinegar
1   pound venison trimmings (it's fine to use a lesser cut than the loin you're buying for this dish), cut into pieces
2   tablespoons olive oil, divided
¼   cup coriander seeds
1   tablespoon black peppercorns
2   bay leaves
2   carrots, cut into medium dice
2   stalks celery, cut into medium dice
1   medium onion, peeled and coarsely chopped
1   quart Veal Stock (page 226)
2   tablespoons heavy cream
1   tablespoon unsalted butter

FOR SERVING:

¼   cup olive oil, divided
1   shallot, peeled and minced
2   teaspoons minced chives
Salt and freshly ground black pepper to taste
2   tablespoons unsalted butter
1   sweet potato, peeled, thinly sliced, and deep-fried, optional garnish
2   fresh figs, cut in half, optional garnish

pepper and keep warm. Cut off the base of the prepared lettuce to separate the leaves. In another sauté pan, warm the lettuce in its vegetable stock.

Remove the meat from the marinade, cut into 8 medallions, season with additional salt, and, one by one, place the medallions in the crust mixture. Turn the meat to coat each piece thoroughly, and shake off any excess.

Preheat oven to 400 degrees F. Heat a large ovenproof skillet, cover the bottom of the pan with the remaining olive oil, and heat until oil begins to smoke. Place the coated medallions in the hot skillet. Working quickly, brown the venison on both sides, being careful not to let the medallions burn. Add the 2 tablespoons of butter to the pan, place the pan in the oven, and cook to the desired degree of doneness (about 3 minutes for medium-rare).

To serve: Place some cabbage in the center of each of 4 dinner plates, top with some lettuce and 2 venison medallions. Spoon some currant sauce over and around the meat, and, if desired, garnish with a fan of deep-fried, thinly sliced sweet potatoes and half a fresh fig.

Wine Match: Here we need to give homage to one of the great game meats. We will turn to a wine looking to meld with the spicy and gamy elements and then, like a gentle wave, wash over these flavors with great ripe fruit. The Rhône Valley grape varieties offer just that — spicy, peppery, and herbal flavors with black currants and gamy notes. Go with the ubiquitous Chateauneuf-du-Pape or a straight 100% Syrah, such as Crozes Hermitage or St. Joseph. You could travel farther south to even spicier blends such as Gigondas. Or, if you want even more fruit, come home and look for a Syrah from California or Washington State, where the classic peppery side of this monumental grape is more evident.

Pepper-Crusted Venison with Lettuce-Cabbage Confit and Black Currant Sauce (recipe on page 124)

Herb-Crusted Chicken Breast with Pasta, Vegetables and Asparagus Sauce

The chefs at Carlos' like to make this dish using whatever fowl is in the kitchen. If the bird has bones, they cook the bird, pull off the meat, and place the meat over the pasta. The sauce can be made using any vegetable you like. It's great any time of year, but if you're looking for something that can be served cold on a hot summer day, try this.

16	pencil-thin asparagus, tops for the dish, bottoms juiced to yield ⅔ cup
1	cup canola oil
	Salt and freshly ground black pepper to taste
1	pound pasta (use farfalle or the shape of your preference)
½	cup olive oil, approximately
4	whole boneless chicken breasts, each split in half
¼	cup chopped parsley
¼	cup minced fresh basil
¼	cup minced fresh tarragon leaves
¼	cup minced fresh chervil
1	yellow squash, cut on the diagonal
1	zucchini, cut on the diagonal
24	shiitake mushrooms, stems removed
4	yellow peppers, cored, seeded, and sliced into rounds
4	green peppers, cored, seeded, and sliced into rounds
1	tablespoon unsalted butter

MAKES 8 SERVINGS

Warm the juice from the asparagus bottoms in a small pot on the stovetop, but do not boil it or the sauce will break. Pour the sauce into a large bowl and slowly whisk in the canola oil, mixing with a hand blender to produce a light, creamy sauce. Season with the salt and pepper.

Cook the pasta according to package directions, drain it, toss with a teaspoon or two of the olive oil to prevent it from sticking, and set aside.

Season the chicken breasts with salt and pepper. Combine the parsley, basil, tarragon, and chervil and sprinkle the mixture over both sides of the chicken, patting to help the seasoning adhere to the chicken.

Place the squash, zucchini, mushrooms, and peppers in a large bowl and cover with 2 tablespoons of the remaining olive oil. Stir to coat. Season the vegetables with additional salt and pepper. Place the vegetables on a hot grill and cook until the grill marks show. (Or place the vegetables under a broiler and lightly brown both sides.)

To cook the chicken: Sauté the prepared chicken breasts in 2 large pans, skin side down, each in 2 tablespoons of the remaining olive oil. Cook until the chicken is lightly browned, about 3 minutes. Turn, cover, and cook for 4 or 5 minutes more, or until browned. Pierce the chicken with a toothpick; when the chicken is done, the juices should run clear. You can make a small slit with a knife to make sure chicken meat has turned white.

Place 1 teaspoon of the remaining olive oil in a large hot pan. Add the cooked pasta and the butter, stir to coat, and top with the grilled vegetables. Toss to combine, and season with additional salt and pepper.

To serve: Place some pasta and vegetables in the center of each of 8 serving plates. Slice the chicken breasts and fan the slices over the pasta. Spoon some warm sauce over chicken and serve.

Wine Match: This simple fare can be accompanied by either a red or white wine. Our pick for white would be a straightforward Sauvignon Blanc from California, with its bright citrus fruit and cleansing acidity to work on the asparagus. For a red, look for juicy, fruit-plentiful, uncomplicated choices. A Côtes-du-Rhône or other southern French wine (from Provence, Minervois, Languedoc-Rousillon) all give you those qualities — plus an earthy oomph to complement the herbs and the always-tricky-to-match asparagus.

Tip: You aren't obligated to use asparagus, although when it's in season, it's a great vegetable for this recipe. If you use another vegetable, use that vegetable's juice in place of asparagus juice.

Wrapped Rabbit Loin with
Spinach, Morels and Sun-Dried Tomatoes

Rabbit is a traditional choice on most French menus. This delicious meat is the perfect centerpiece for a hearty dinner with flavors that enhance every side dish. This recipe is a favorite with our guests. If you substitute lamb for the rabbit, you'll have a terrific meal, but we love it just the way it is.

8   loins of rabbit, cleaned
Salt and white pepper to taste
16   slices pancetta
¼   cup olive oil, divided
2   full rabbit rib portions, quartered and frenched (all meat scraped off the bones), optional
2   tablespoons unsalted butter, divided
8   cups fresh baby spinach
24   morel mushrooms, whole
12   sun-dried tomatoes
8   chives, cut into 3-inch strips

MAKES 4 SERVINGS

Lightly season the rabbit loin pieces with salt and pepper on both sides. Cover the loin pieces with the pancetta slices and secure with toothpicks. Heat a large skillet and add 3 tablespoons of the olive oil. Cook the rabbit loins over high heat on both sides to the desired degree of doneness. When the pancetta is brown and crispy, the meat will probably be medium or medium-rare. Brown the meat off the rib sections, if you're using them, and keep them warm.

In a separate large skillet, melt half the butter and wilt the spinach. Season with additional salt and pepper. Drain any excess moisture. Keep the spinach warm in the pan.

In a small pan over high heat, melt the remaining butter and sauté the mushrooms.

In a small sauté pan, heat the remaining olive oil, add the sun-dried tomatoes, and heat through.

To serve: Slice the rabbit loins. Place a 4-inch ring mold in the center of a large dinner plate, line the bottom of the ring with a layer of wilted spinach, and top with some sun-dried tomatoes. Remove the ring mold and arrange a portion of the rabbit slices over the tomatoes. Top with a quarter rack of rib section. Insert 2 chive strips between the rib bones, and surround with 6 morels. Repeat for each of the four portions.

Wine Match: Fruit presence in the wine is very important here. There's gaminess from the rabbit, a lot of substance from the pancetta, and earthiness from the tomatoes and morels, so we need to pick a full-bodied wine loaded with fruit. Our first instinct is to go with a Rhône Valley variety, but the bacon in the dish makes the decision: This is a perfect dish for a Zinfandel. But don't go for a full-throttle, alcoholic example. We don't need Port wine here — look for something well balanced. Zinfandel is always fruit-laden.

Tip: The rabbit rib portions are essentially a garnish, and a cut that can be far more difficult to find than rabbit loins. For home presentation, they can be omitted.

Beef Tenderloin with Potatoes, Vegetables and Chocolate Wine Sauce

Most people wouldn't think that chocolate could play any role in a savory sauce. But Carlos' chefs bring inventiveness and a great sense of cuisine to every dish. With no patrons until dinner, lunchtime becomes a good opportunity for them to experiment. This recipe is an example. Don't overlook the potatoes; they're terrific paired with many entrées. Although we serve them in a fancy ring mold, they are just as delicious scooped out of the pan with a large spoon or spatula.

1½ cups dry red wine
½ cup sugar
¼ cup bittersweet chocolate morsels (we prefer the French discs)
2 tablespoons demiglace (available at specialty stores)
Salt and freshly ground black pepper to taste
8 baking potatoes, peeled and sliced paper-thin with a mandoline
1 cup grated Asiago cheese
3 cups heavy cream
8 filet mignon steaks (or sirloin or New York strip steaks), about 6 ounces each
1 teaspoon extra-virgin olive oil
40 pencil-thin asparagus spears, tips only (see Note)
16 baby carrots (see Note)
Vegetable oil, to coat

MAKES 8 SERVINGS

To make the sauce: Place the wine and sugar in a medium saucepan over medium heat. Stir to combine, bring to a simmer, reduce by half and slowly add the chocolate as you reduce, stirring to combine. Add the demiglace, stir, and season with the salt and pepper. The sauce should have a syrupy consistency. It can be made up to 2 days in advance and stored in the refrigerator. Warm just before serving.

To make the potatoes: Preheat oven to 375 degrees F. Using a shallow, oven-proof baking dish, about 5½ x 12 x 2 inches, alternately layer the potatoes and the cheese, lightly seasoning with additional salt and pepper, and starting and ending with the potatoes. When the pan is three-quarters full, pour over the cream until it just covers the potatoes. Place in the oven for approximately 1 hour, or until golden brown on top. Place the potatoes, still in their pan, on the bottom shelf of the refrigerator for at least 2 hours (or as long as 1 day) before serving. Remove the potatoes from the refrigerator and, while they are cold, cut them with a ring mold of similar size to the steaks. Keep the cut potatoes out of the refrigerator.

To make the beef: Preheat the oven to 500 degrees F. Coat the steaks with oil, season with salt and pepper, and place on a very hot grill or under the broiler. Char each side and the ends, then place in the oven for 5 minutes for medium rare, an additional 4 minutes for medium. (Keep the beef warm while it sits for a few minutes.)

To prepare the vegetables: Coat the asparagus and carrots in oil and grill in a vegetable basket or on aluminum foil pierced a few times with a fork. Grill or broil for 5 to 7 minutes, or until asparagus is slightly charred.

To serve: Reduce the oven temperature to 400 degrees F. Place the cut potatoes on a cookie sheet and heat in the preheated oven until they are warmed through. Place on serving plates, top each with a steak, surround with vegetables, and drizzle the top with the warm sauce.

Note: You may substitute the vegetable(s) of your choice.

Wine Match: This is for you, Cabernet lovers! Choose your style. You can look for a fruit-focused Sonoma or a Paso Robles wine, or you can choose a tasty mocha-accented Napa Valley wine. If you like a little peppery flavor in your wine, try something from Washington State, Australia, or Spain. Those varietals rely on American oak for their maturation. The oak imparts a nice essence and adds a delicious chocolaty accent to the wine. Try a different wine each time you prepare this dish.

Squab with Root Vegetables and Shallot-Sherry Gastrique

This preparation really brings out the squab flavor, but it would be just as delicious with duck (but a little too heavy for chicken). *Gastrique* is a French term for a sauce that combines sugar and vinegar. Although there is no vinegar in this recipe, the sherry acts as the vinegar component. Be sure to use cream sherry, which has a smoother, richer flavor, not cooking sherry. Make the sauce a day or two ahead and marinate the squab overnight.

GASTRIQUE (SAUCE):

1	tablespoon unsalted butter
6	large shallots, peeled and cut in medium slices
1	cup cream sherry
4	cups Veal Stock (page 226)

Salt and freshly ground black pepper to taste

SQUAB AND MARINADE:

12	squab (each portion is 4 deboned breast halves and 4 legs)
1	cup dry red wine
1	tablespoon black peppercorns
6	bay leaves
6	juniper berries, crushed
6	sprigs thyme
½	cup dried lavender

VEGETABLES AND SERVING:

30	baby carrots, peeled
12	baby turnips, peeled
12	baby beets, greens removed and reserved

Salt and freshly ground black pepper to taste

3	tablespoons vegetable oil
2	tablespoons unsalted butter
½	cup honey

Tomato Oil (page 214), optional garnish
Basil Oil (page 213), optional garnish

12	cherry tomatoes, halved, for garnish

Fried leeks (page 22), optional garnish

MAKES 6 SERVINGS

To make the gastrique: Melt the butter in a large pan over medium heat and cook the shallots in the hot butter until they are browned. (This releases the sugars and makes the sauce sweeter.) Deglaze the pan with the sherry and cook for about 8 minutes, until the liquid is reduced by half. Add the Veal Stock, stir, and reduce the sauce until it coats the back of a spoon, about 10 to 15 minutes. Season with salt and pepper, let cool to room temperature, then refrigerate. Before serving, reheat over low heat. Adjust seasonings.

To prepare the squab: Place the breasts and legs in a glass, plastic, or stainless steel container. Add the wine, peppercorns, bay leaves, juniper berries, thyme sprigs, and lavender. Stir to coat meat. Cover and refrigerate overnight.

To make the vegetables: Cook the carrots and turnips only until they are fork-tender. Boil the beets with their skin for about 20 minutes, then remove them from the water, let them cool slightly, and peel them. Cut the beets and turnips in half.

To serve: Preheat oven to 400 degrees F. Remove the squab from the marinade. Discard all the liquid, and, using a brush, remove everything but the lavender pieces. Season the skin side of the squab with salt and pepper. Heat the oil in two large pans over high heat, sear the squab breasts, skin side down, until they are brown and crispy. Turn them over and place the pans in the oven for 2 minutes. Meanwhile, season the skin side of the legs with additional salt and pepper. Remove the pan from the oven, let the breasts sit in a warm spot, and brown the legs in the same pans used for the breasts. Then turn the legs and place them in the oven for 2 minutes. Squab cooks very fast and is best when served medium rare. (Remember: it's fowl, not a chicken, and its dark meat does not need to be cooked as thoroughly as chicken. If it is overcooked, it will be dry and tough.) Remove from the oven and let rest on a cutting board.

In another pan, heat the butter and honey until melted. Add the prepared carrots, beets, and turnips, stir to coat the vegetables, and heat through. Add the beet greens, toss until they wilt, about 2 or 3 minutes, and adjust seasoning.

Arrange a portion of vegetables in a half-circle on each of six serving plates. Spoon a few tablespoons of the gastrique in front of the vegetables, prop 2 legs over the vegetables, slice 2 breast pieces in half, and lean the breast slices over the legs.

Drizzle the outside of the vegetables and squab with Tomato Oil, then dot the circle with Basil Oil. Garnish each serving with 4 tomato halves. Top with a small pile of Fried Leeks.

Wine Match: Squab is our chef's favorite game meat. The key to a successful wine pairing here is to balance the gaminess of the meat and the lavender aromatics without overwhelming the bird. A syrah or syrah-based wine works very well. The innate

richness of fruit in this varietal allied with abundant aromatics that include lavender just swims on the surface of this dish. Look for a fruit-driven syrah. Stay away from powerful or over-oaked wines.

Tip: Never marinate meat in an aluminum bowl. It causes a chemical reaction that will distort the flavor. Use a bowl that's nonreactive, such as glass, plastic, or stainless steel.

Tip: Wear gloves when handling beets to prevent staining of your hands.

Grilled Strip Steak with Fava Beans, Baby Carrots, Tomatoes and Mushrooms

Sometimes the simplest recipes turn out to be the favorites. We think you'll find that's the case with this delicious strip steak. Steak and "frites" have been a standby in fine French restaurants, including ours, for as long as we can remember. Use this recipe with your favorite cuts of meat and the vegetables of your choice. Look for our Pommes Frites recipe (page 171) for a perfect side dish.

RED WINE SAUCE:

- 1 pound beef trimmings
- 1 large carrot, cut into medium dice
- 1 medium onion, cut into medium dice
- 1 to 2 stalks celery, cut into medium dice
- 1 pound wild mushrooms, coarsely chopped
- ½ cup dried mushrooms, any variety
- ½ teaspoon black peppercorns
- 2 bay leaves
- 5 sprigs fresh thyme
- 2 cups red wine
- 4 cups veal or beef stock

VEGETABLES:

- 2 tablespoons unsalted butter
- ½ cup fava beans, peeled and blanched
- ½ cup baby carrots, quartered and blanched
- ½ cup currant tomatoes
- 2 shallots, minced
- 2 tablespoons minced chives
- Salt and freshly ground black pepper to taste

STEAKS:

- 4 New York strip steaks, each about 10 ounces
- Salt and freshly ground black pepper to taste

MAKES 4 SERVINGS

To prepare the red wine sauce: Brown the meat trimmings in a medium pot. Add the diced carrot, onion, and celery, and stir until soft, about 10 minutes. Add the mushrooms and continue to sauté. (The dried mushrooms will rehydrate as liquid is added.) Add the peppercorns, bay leaves, and thyme, and stir until all the vegetables are browned, about 8 to 10 minutes. Add the wine and reduce the mixture until it is almost dry. Add the veal stock and simmer until reduced by half. Adjust seasoning, strain, skim off any fat, and refrigerate the sauce (which can be made up to 2 days in advance).

To make the vegetables: Melt the butter in a medium skillet over medium-low heat. Add the beans and carrots, heat through, and gently stir in the tomatoes, shallots, and chives. Cook just until warm. Season with salt and pepper.

Season the steaks with salt and pepper, and grill or broil them to desired doneness.

To serve: Place small mound of vegetables on each of four large dinner plates. Top each with a cooked steak and spoon some sauce around. This is delicious served with Soft Herb Polenta (page 170) or Pommes Frites (page 171).

Wine Match: Beef, especially a prime cut with plenty of marbling, such as a strip steak, begs for a tannic wine such as a Cabernet Sauvignon. You may opt to go the way of the French and serve a Bordeaux or settle for America's most famed varietal by serving a Napa Valley wine. Choose your budget and enjoy one of the simplest and most satisfying wine-food combinations.

Tip: If you use a canned broth, the sauce will be much thinner, no matter how much you reduce it. But the taste will still be great.

Tip: You can used shelled edamames (boiled soybeans) to replace the fava beans.

Chicken Breast with Braised Belgian Endive

This hearty dish is especially appealing in the fall or winter — and the celery root purée could become one of your regular side dishes. We would say the same about the endive. Although it could be omitted from this recipe, we love the foie gras cream. (Because it will be melted and puréed, your specialty store may have some scraps that will do fine.)

3 medium celery roots, peeled, cut in quarters, then cut into large dice

2 quarts whole milk

6 Belgian endive, trimmed of brown or frayed leaves, cut in half lengthwise

5 tablespoons vegetable oil, divided

Salt and freshly ground black pepper to taste

2 tablespoons sugar

½ cup white wine

1 cup chicken stock

3 cups heavy cream, divided

6 ounces foie gras (trimmings or pieces are fine)

1 tablespoon Red Wine Syrup (page 227)

3 boneless chicken breasts, skin on and split in half, about 3 pounds total

¾ cup chopped tarragon leaves

Fried sweet potato (page 22), optional garnish

MAKES 6 SERVINGS

Heat the celery roots and milk in a large pot over medium heat. (The milk tends to foam and boil over, so shake the pot occasionally to settle the foam.) Cook approximately 30 minutes, or until the celery roots are fork-tender.

Meanwhile, prepare the endive. Preheat the oven to 400 degrees F. Sear the endive in a pan with 1 tablespoon of the vegetable oil. Season with salt and pepper. When the endive is brown on both sides, add the sugar and stir to coat. Add the wine to deglaze the pan, then add the chicken stock. Let cook for about 5 minutes, turn the endive, and cook for 2 more minutes. Place the pan with the endive in the oven and cook until fork-tender, about 5 to 6 minutes.

When the celery root is finished cooking, strain and purée in a food processor. Slowly add about 1 cup of the cream, checking the texture. You want the purée to have the texture of light mashed potatoes, not to be runny. Do not overwork.

While the endive is cooking, place the foie gras and remaining cream in a saucepan and, at a very low simmer, let it steep for about 30 minutes. The foie gras will begin to slowly break down and the cream and the fat from the foie gras will emulsify. Let the mixture cool, then purée until smooth. Season with the Red Wine Syrup.

Season the chicken breasts with salt and pepper and sprinkle both sides with tarragon, patting down the leaves so they adhere, until thickly coated. Sear the skin of the breasts in a hot pan with the remaining vegetable oil until crisp and caramelized, about 3 or 4 minutes. Turn the chicken and cook on the second side for 4 or 5 minutes. Add more oil if needed. Remove from the pan, and cut the chicken on the bias into 3 pieces.

To serve: Place some celery root purée in the center of each of six dinner plates. Cut each piece of endive in half again and, from 4 endive pieces on each plate, create a square frame around the purée. Place the cut chicken over the purée, and top with some fried sweet potato.

Wine Match: This homey dish features great aromatics with the tarragon and earthy richness in the sauce. We'll make this sparkle with a lively, clean, mineral, white-wine influence. We would choose a Pinot Blanc from Alsace. This is a relatively uncomplicated crisp white wine with a pretty wildflower nose that would contrast with the flavors in this dish and complement the aromas.

Tip: If you're in a hurry, put the celery root purée on a plate, top with chicken breast, and place the halved endive next to it.

CARLOS' SPECIALS

Owning Carlos' has enabled us to travel the world in search of cuisines and recipes that might find their way onto our menu. We've also been the guest chefs for many cooking trips. Our menus for these trips are based on available ingredients for each travel destination and for the season of the year. And many recipes come from ideas that we adapt from our monthly cooking classes.

Our many destinations, both domestic and foreign, have allowed us to share food experiences with our patrons. We create culinary memories wherever we go and try to make them extensions of the memories we hope to create for each of our guests' visits to Carlos'.

In this chapter, you will find a sampling of some of the favorites from our travels. There were many to choose from, but these were among our most requested recipes. We hope they will inspire you to visit the "world" of Carlos' cooking.

carlos' specials

the recipes

LAMB LOIN PACKAGES WITH VEGETABLES AND SHERRY-SHALLOT SAUCE   140

LOBSTER WITH CURRY LEEK "SPAGHETTINI"   143

PAN-SEARED SCALLOPS WITH CHANTERELLES, SPINACH AND LEMONGRASS SAUCE   144

RACK OF LAMB WITH ROSEMARY JUS, GARLIC MASHED POTATOES AND VEGETABLES   147

GLAZED VENISON MEDALLIONS WITH SAUTÉED BABY CARROTS AND HERB POLENTA   148

Lamb Loin Packages with Vegetables and Sherry-Shallot Sauce

This recipe is more challenging than most in this book. None of the steps are difficult in themselves, but they do require more time and patience. The results, however, will be well worth your efforts. You will savor the flavor of the lamb wrapped within its blanket (although the lamb loin by itself would be delicious, too). Combine each bite with the textures produced from side dishes and the flavor of the sauce and you'll have a taste sensation. Mashed Potatoes or Sautéed Mushrooms and Potatoes (page 170) would be good side-dish accompaniments.

3 small to medium lamb loins, each cut in half

Salt and freshly ground black pepper to taste

1 tablespoon canola oil

1 tablespoon grainy mustard

6 sheets feuille de brick or phyllo dough (see Note)

2 tablespoons Clarified Butter, approximately (page 220)

12 large basil leaves

1 zucchini, thinly sliced lengthwise

1 yellow squash, thinly sliced lengthwise

1 medium purple potato, thinly sliced

½ small eggplant, thinly sliced

Salt and freshly ground black pepper to taste

½ pound Asiago cheese, grated

1 roasted red bell pepper, peeled and halved

1 roasted yellow bell pepper, peeled and halved

SWEET SHERRY-SHALLOT SAUCE:

20 shallots, peeled and sliced

2 tablespoons canola oil

½ cup sugar

1 bottle (750 ml) cooking sherry

3 quarts Veal Stock (page 226)

MAKES 6 SERVINGS

Season the lamb with salt and pepper. Heat the oil in a very hot, medium-size pan, and sear the lamb for no more than 1 minute per side. Let cool to room temperature for a few minutes, and brush with grainy mustard. Brush the feuille de brick with some of the Clarified Butter. Place 1 basil leaf, a piece of the chilled lamb, and another basil leaf on top of the feuille de brick. Wrap as you would an eggroll and refrigerate until ready for use.

Preheat oven to 350 degrees F. Place the zucchini, squash, potato, and eggplant on a sheet pan, drizzle with more of the Clarified Butter, season with the salt and pepper, and roast in the oven for about 5 minutes. Place the roasted vegetables, with half the cheese scattered among them, in a layer in a shallow baking pan. Top with the red and yellow pepper halves, and place the remaining cheese on top of the peppers. Bake for 15 to 20 minutes, or until the cheese on top melts. Refrigerate. Cut into about 6 even pieces. When ready to serve, reheat in oven.

To prepare the sauce: Brown the shallots in the oil in a large saucepan for about 15 minutes. Add the sugar and cook for about 5 minutes, until further browned. Add the sherry and reduce by half. Add the stock and reduce over medium heat until the liquid coats the back of a spoon, skimming the surface periodically. Keep the sauce warm.

To finish the lamb: Preheat oven to 500 degrees F. Coat a sheet pan with the remaining Clarified Butter, place the lamb packages on the sheet, and roast in the oven for 8 to 10 minutes. Let rest for 2 to 3 minutes and slice in half diagonally. Serve with the vegetable-cheese mixture, reduction sauce, and a side dish of your choice.

Note: "Feuille de brick" is a crêpe-like product. It is sometimes sold with the last word spelled "brix." The closest alternative would be to use buttered phyllo sheets to wrap the lamb.

Wine Match: The classic pairing of lamb and wine would dictate a red Bordeaux from the Right Bank. The complexity of the wine from this region mixes well with the flavorful lamb. It's important to find a wine with some tannins. Tannins mix very well with the protein and fats in lamb and other fine cuts of meat. The tannins give the impression of almost softening the meat. Look for a wine that has rich black currant, blackberry, and plum flavors. A fine St. Emilion or Pomerol would be the wine of choice.

Tip: Get friendly with your fine-dining establishment and the people there *might* help you procure hard-to-find or exotic foods.

Lobster with Curry Leek "Spaghettini"

These tender pieces of lobster are right at home nestled on the lightly curried leeks, sliced to resemble angel-hair pasta. The tarragon flavor is subtle. Lobsters need to be alive as long as possible before their meat is used. If you don't want to do the deed yourself, your fishmonger will do it for you and will cut the lobster into the pieces you want. Be sure to use the lobster meat within a few hours.

LOBSTERS:

6 tablespoons vegetable oil
6 lobsters, about 1½ pounds each

LEEK "SPAGHETTINI":

3 leeks, white parts only, thoroughly cleaned and cut into julienne strips
1½ cups heavy cream
¼ teaspoon curry powder
3 large carrots, cut into tiny balls (with a small melon baller) or small dice
1 tablespoon minced chives
1 large shallot, minced
Salt and freshly ground black pepper to taste

FOR SERVING:

4 tablespoons (½ stick) unsalted butter
Salt and freshly ground black pepper to taste
¼ cup whole tarragon leaves, loosely packed
Beurre Blanc (page 220)
Fried leeks and/or fried carrots (page 22), for garnish
Basil Oil (page 213), for garnish

MAKES 6 SERVINGS

To prepare the lobsters: Preheat the oven to 400 degrees F. Heat the oil in a large ovenproof skillet, quickly sear the lobster claws and tails on both sides, the meat still in the shells, and bake in the oven for approximately 7 minutes, or until the shells turn bright red and the tail meat looks opaque. Do not overcook the meat. Remove from the oven and place under cold running water. Cut the shells away with sharp scissors or a knife, and remove the meat, keeping the tail whole for when you arrange the plates.

To make the leek "spaghettini": Cut off the white bulb and the bottom of the leeks and discard the outer dry leaves. Cut the leek into extremely thin julienne strips, so they resemble angel-hair pasta. Place the leek strips in a large pot and cover with cold, salted water by about 2 inches, bring to a boil, and cook for approximately 2 minutes, until the strips have softened. Drain the strips and place them in ice water to stop the cooking. When cool, squeeze out water, and set aside.

Pour the cream in a large pan over medium-high heat, add the leeks and curry, bring to a boil, and cook about 2 minutes. Add the carrots, chives, and shallot, season with salt and pepper, and cook for 5 minutes or until the sauce clings to the leeks. Adjust seasonings.

To serve: Melt the butter in a large skillet and toss the lobster pieces in the hot butter. Add a small amount of salt and pepper and the tarragon leaves. Stir just until leaves are wilted and the lobster pieces are coated. Place a small mound of the prepared leek strips in the center of each of six dinner plates. Then arrange lobster pieces around the leeks on each plate so that the pieces look like a whole lobster. Place a lobster claw on each side of the top of the mound of leeks, place the tail toward the bottom of the mound, and lay the tail shell on the plate below. Spoon a few tablespoons of Beurre Blanc sauce around. Garnish each plate with a few pieces of Fried Leeks and/or Fried Carrots, and dot the outer rim of each plate with Basil Oil.

Wine Match: Curry begs for a wine with clean, firm fruit flavors but not the dissonance that would result from oak influence. We need a full-bodied wine, one with plenty of aromatics, to stand up to the richness of the dish. The varietals that come to mind are Marsanne and Roussane. These are cultivated in France's Rhône Valley and can be found in white Chateauneuf-du-Pape (yes, there is such a thing). California and Australia also produce wine from these grapes, as do other areas of southern France. If you can't find these wines, look for a Pinot Gris from Alsace, France, or Oregon.

Tip: A good way to wash leeks, which can be very gritty, is to cut the julienne before washing. Place the strips in a large bowl of cold water, slosh the leeks in the water, and watch the grit fall to the bottom of the bowl. Discard the water and repeat the process.

Pan-Seared Scallops with Chanterelles, Spinach and Lemongrass Sauce

This dish can be ready in about 40 minutes. Resist the temptation to make all 16 scallops in a large pan. If you put too many scallops in the pan at the same time, they get crowded, rub against each other, and steam instead of sauté. This makes them soggy and tough, and it zaps them of their sweet flavor. Making them in batches of four really goes quickly. We highly recommend using dry-packed sea scallops, as these little gems have an incredible texture. For an appetizer portion, use two scallops as pictured.

SCALLOPS:

16 jumbo sea scallops, about 2 ounces each
Salt and freshly ground black pepper to taste
¼ cup vegetable oil, divided
1 tablespoon minced chives, divided
1 tablespoon minced shallots, divided
2 tablespoons unsalted butter, softened
2 cups chopped chanterelle mushrooms
1 pound baby spinach
20 thin asparagus tips, blanched
1 teaspoon Garlic Herb Butter (page 221)
8 cherry tomatoes, halved

LEMONGRASS SAUCE:

1 quart heavy cream
5 stalks fresh lemongrass, crushed and cut into slices
Juice of 2 small limes (about ¼ cup)
¼ cup Simple Syrup (page 228)
Salt and freshly ground black pepper to taste

MAKES 4 SERVINGS

Season the scallops with salt and pepper, and let them sit at room temperature for 5 minutes.

While the scallops are sitting, make the lemongrass sauce: Pour the heavy cream into a large, heavy-bottomed pot, add the prepared lemongrass, and simmer. Reduce the volume by half, strain, and add the lime juice and Simple Syrup. Season with salt and pepper. Keep the sauce warm.

Now resume preparing the scallops. Preheat the oven to 425 degrees F. Heat 1 tablespoon of the oil in a medium-size, heavy-duty skillet. The pan should be very hot but not smoking. Sear the scallops in batches of four, for about 1 minute on the first side, until the scallops are browned with a crust, and for about 1 minute on the second side. You'll probably need a second tablespoon of oil midway through the batches. Place the finished scallops on a jelly roll pan lined with foil. When all the scallops are finished, place the pan in the oven for 4 minutes, or until the scallops are translucent. Toss the scallops with half the chives, half the shallots, and the butter to create a sheen on the scallops.

Sauté the mushrooms in a large, heavy-bottomed pan in another tablespoon of the oil. Sprinkle with additional salt and pepper, and toss the mushrooms until they are fully cooked. Remove the mushrooms, keep them warm, and add another tablespoon of oil to the same pan. Add the spinach, cook until just wilted, and remove to a warm spot. Add the asparagus tips to the same pan just to warm them, for about 1 minute. Sprinkle lightly with the remaining minced chives and shallots. Add the Garlic Herb Butter. Toss all vegetables and adjust seasonings to taste.

To serve: Ladle a small amount of sauce on the bottom of each of four serving plates. Place a portion of mushrooms in the center of each plate and top with a portion of the spinach and asparagus tips. Place 4 scallops on the spinach in a 2-by-2 pattern, insert 4 asparagus spears between the scallops, and place the 4 tomato halves next to the scallops.

Note: Lemongrass is a stalk-like ingredient sold fresh in Asian markets and many supermarkets. It releases its flavor when cut or bruised.

Wine Match: The lemongrass and mushrooms in this recipe grab our attention, and several varietals of wine come to mind. However, our choice would be to stay high-toned and look for a complex white wine, such as an Alsace Pinot Gris or a Spanish wine, Rueda.

Rack of Lamb with Rosemary Jus, Garlic Mashed Potatoes and Vegetables

A while back, a favorite customer waxed poetic about a lamb dish from a recent vacation. She described how the crust of herbs and bread crumbs created an incredible halo for the meat, how the mashed potatoes had a delicate lacing of garlic, and how it was served with a bouquet of vegetables that she blended with the potatoes to make a perfect mouthful of food. From that sensual description, we developed this recipe. She gave us the highest compliment, saying that we had exceeded her expectations. Over the years, we have created many new and exciting ways to serve lamb, but we return to this recipe time and again. Prepare it in advance to help the bread crumbs adhere to the lamb.

LAMB AND CRUST:

2 racks of lamb, frenched (see Note)
Kosher salt and freshly ground black pepper to taste
2 tablespoons canola oil, approximately
½ cup fine bread crumbs
½ cup cornflake crumbs
¼ cup freshly chopped rosemary
1 tablespoon salt
1 teaspoon freshly ground black pepper
1 clove minced garlic
2 tablespoons unsalted butter, melted
3 to 4 tablespoons Dijon mustard

JUS:

1 large onion, coarsely chopped
1 medium carrot, coarsely chopped
2 medium stalks celery, coarsely chopped
2 tablespoons canola oil
3 cloves garlic, smashed
1 tablespoon black peppercorns
2 bay leaves
½ cup sherry
2 sprigs rosemary

MAKES 4 SERVINGS

Season the meat on all surfaces with salt and pepper. Heat a large, nonstick skillet until it's smoking and add the oil. One rack at a time, lightly brown all sides of the meat in the skillet. Let the racks cool. You may need additional oil.

To prepare the crust: Combine the bread crumbs, cornflake crumbs, rosemary, salt, pepper, garlic, and melted butter, making sure that the crumbs are evenly coated with the butter. The mixture should be moist enough to stick together.

When the outer surface of the meat has cooled, brush liberally with the mustard and press the prepared crust mixture onto the mustard-covered lamb. Coat well, patting as necessary, and make sure the crust is thick and even. Cover the lamb tightly with plastic wrap and refrigerate at least 1 hour, or overnight.

To make the jus: Sauté the onion, carrot, and celery in the canola oil until the vegetables are lightly browned. Add the garlic, peppercorns, and bay leaves, stir to combine, and add the sherry. Cook, reducing until nearly all the liquid has evaporated. Add 1 sprig of the rosemary and the Lamb Stock, and cook over medium heat, stirring occasionally until reduced by one-quarter. Skim any fat off the surface. Strain the reduced liquid and keep warm until ready to serve. (Or you can make this a day in advance, refrigerate until it's ready for use, and reheat before serving.) About 15 minutes before serving, remove any excess fat from the warm liquid and add the second sprig of rosemary. Season the liquid with salt and pepper.

Preheat oven to 400 degrees F. Place the prepared lamb on a metal rack in a roasting pan, and roast for 20 to 30 minutes, or until the internal temperature reads 135 degrees F. on a meat thermometer for medium-rare. Make sure the crust does not burn. Remove the lamb from the oven and let it rest for 5 minutes before cutting.

While the lamb is resting, finish the Garlic Mashed Potatoes and prepare the vegetables. Warm the tomatoes in 2 tablespoons of the lamb jus in a small pan. In another pan, sauté the mushrooms in the canola oil until lightly brown, remove from the heat, add the butter, and season with salt and pepper. Warm the haricots verts in the same pan used for the mushrooms.

To serve: Place a three-inch ring mold in the center of a serving plate. Fill the ring three-quarters full with the mashed potatoes, top with the sautéed mushrooms, and arrange the tomatoes and the haricots verts around the potatoes. Cut each rack of lamb in half, then cut in half again, and lean the chops on either side of potatoes,

recipe continued on page 148

2 quarts Lamb Stock (page 225) or
beef stock
Kosher salt and freshly ground black
pepper to taste

POTATOES, VEGETABLES, AND SERVING:

Roasted Garlic Mashed Potatoes with
Dijon Mustard (page 169)
24 red grape tomatoes
6 shiitake mushrooms, cleaned and
thinly sliced
1 tablespoon canola oil
1 tablespoon unsalted butter
Kosher salt and freshly ground black
pepper to taste
32 haricots verts (thin green beans),
blanched

intertwining the bones over the top. Remove the rosemary sprigs and bay leaves from the jus and drizzle the remaining liquid around the meat, potatoes, and vegetables.

Note: Frenching a rack of lamb means removing the excess flesh from the ends of the bones so the bones are clean. Your butcher can do this for you.

Wine Match: This classic dish can be combined with any of several red wines. The complexity of the lamb done on the bone asks for a Cabernet blend because of its good tannic structure. Bordeaux comes to mind, although California has plenty to offer in terms of blends. The "Meritage" and other so-called proprietary blends have the layered flavors that enhance the simplicity of this preparation and yet marry well with its richness. When looking for a selection, stay away from overripe, highly alcoholic styles. For safety, just go to the Bordeaux. For affordability, look to Chile or Argentina. Even a 100 percent Cabernet from these areas can work well.

Tip: "Cooking sherry" and "sherry" often mean very different products. Cooking sherry usually contains additives, such as sugar, salt, and preservatives, and is not intended as a beverage. Sherry is meant as a beverage and produces superior results as a cooking ingredient.

Glazed Venison Medallions with Sautéed Baby Carrots and Herb Polenta
Venison is a delicious, moist, flavorful game meat. Never had it before? Try it. You'll be glad you did. This recipe must be prepared a day in advance.

VENISON AND MARINADE:

1 cup olive oil
2 cups red wine
10 juniper berries
3 star anise
4 cloves garlic, smashed
1 stalk celery, coarsely chopped
1 carrot, coarsely chopped
½ medium Spanish onion, coarsely
chopped
5 sprigs thyme
1 tablespoon black peppercorns

MAKES 4 SERVINGS

To prepare the venison and marinade: Combine the olive oil, wine, juniper berries, star anise, garlic, celery, carrot, onion, thyme, and peppercorns in a shallow glass pan. Place the venison medallions in the pan and marinate for at least 24 hours. Remove the medallions from the marinade when you're ready to cook the meat, and season them with salt and pepper.

To make the herb polenta: Bring the chicken stock to boil in a medium pot, add the salt and pepper, reduce the heat to low, and mix in the polenta, whisking to remove any lumps. The polenta should thicken to a consistency of loose oatmeal. Add the butter, a few pieces at a time and stir until melted. Add the cream and stir to combine. Mix in the Parmesan cheese. Remove from the heat and fold in the chopped herbs. Adjust seasoning. Keep the polenta warm in any of several ways: Place the pot with the polenta into a larger pot of warm water so that the water comes halfway up the polenta pot; place the polenta

8   medallions of venison loin, each
    about 4 ounces
Salt and freshly ground black pepper
    to taste

SOFT HERB POLENTA:
3   cups Chicken Stock (page 225)
Salt and white pepper to taste
1   cup instant polenta
8   tablespoons (1 stick) unsalted
    butter, cut into pieces
¼   cup heavy cream
¼   cup grated Parmesan cheese
⅔   cup mixed herbs (rosemary, chives,
    basil, chervil, tarragon, parsley,
    etc.), finely chopped (see Note)

VENISON GLAZE:
1   tablespoon dark brown sugar
½   cup light corn syrup
⅓   cup pineapple juice
2   tablespoons bourbon
Salt and freshly ground black pepper
    to taste
¼   teaspoon cayenne pepper
1   clove garlic, smashed and minced
¼   cup vegetable oil
½   teaspoon Worcestershire sauce

VEGETABLES:
1   cup baby carrots
1   tablespoon unsalted butter
½   cup currant tomatoes
Salt and white pepper to taste

in the top of a double boiler with hot water in the bottom; or cover the polenta and place it in a warm oven. Stir before serving.

To make the venison glaze: Whisk together the sugar, corn syrup, and pineapple juice. Add the bourbon and stir to incorporate. Mix in the salt, pepper, cayenne pepper, garlic, vegetable oil, and Worcestershire sauce. Place in a small pot over low heat and reduce to thicken (watching carefully to be sure that the glaze does not burn). Stir often. Remove from heat, adjust seasoning, and let cool, but whisk before serving. (This can be made 1 day in advance and kept refrigerated. If so, reheat and whisk before serving. Remember: You'll need some of this glaze for the vegetables, as directed below.)

To prepare the vegetables: Blanch the carrots in boiling water, then plunge them into ice water to stop the cooking. Just before serving, melt the butter in a medium pan and reheat the carrots in the melted butter over low heat. When the carrots are warm, add the tomatoes and 1 to 2 tablespoons (more, if you wish) of warm venison glaze. Stir the carrots to coat with the glaze. Season with salt and pepper.

To cook the venison: Heat a grill and wipe it with oil. Grill the venison (or it could be broiled) on one side, turn the meat, brush the cooked side with glaze, turn again and brush with more glaze. Cook to desired doneness, 3 to 4 minutes per side with a medium flame for medium-rare.

To serve: Place a medium ring mold in the center of a large plate, and fill the mold with herb polenta. Remove the mold and place 2 medallions, side by side, on the polenta. Brush with glaze. Surround with a portion of the carrots and tomatoes, and dot with additional glaze, if desired.

Note: Use any combination of herbs, finely chopped and compacted to measure ⅔ cup. You do not have to use all the herbs listed, but if you use rosemary, chop it separately, because the texture of the leaves requires finer chopping.

Wine Match: Because this is an aromatic game dish with a sweet edge coming from the glaze, we need a red wine with gaminess and spiciness to stand up to this multi-layered creation. Chateauneuf-du-Pape, with its complex blend of Syrah, Grenache, and other grapes, offers just that. Look for the great vintages of 2001 or 2000. For an edgier combination, look for a Bandol from Provence. Mourvedre is the main grape here and it has the backbone and flavor that we're looking for.

One month after opening the restaurant, Carlos ordered 25 large pizzas to be delivered for the employees' meals. The deliveryman arrived with the huge boxes. Debbie answered the door and said, "You've got to be kidding. This is a French restaurant. Why would we want these pizzas?" She sent him on his way. About an hour later, Carlos came in and asked, "Where are the pizzas I ordered for the staff meals?" They had to call the pizza place and have them redelivered.

Today, staff meals are better. Every day at about 2:30 p.m., our staff stops chopping vegetables, baking pastries, preparing soups and sauces, and setting tables and enjoys a quick but fresh, homemade meal that will hold their hunger until at least 10:00 that night. This meal is prepared by a different cook each day, and the staff members themselves take turns deciding what to make on a particular day, based on the odds and ends that are left in the kitchen. A good chef orders well enough so that little will go to waste. For the staff meals, our chef and cooks utilize cuts that we wouldn't serve to our patrons. For example, they might make a Beef Bourguignon stew from the leftover cuts of beef, as in the Beef Bourguignon recipe in this chapter. Or they could make a delicious fish soup from the fish trimmings cut away from the more regal pieces we serve to customers. But it's more than just a meal. It gives our staff a few moments to relax and socialize with their fellow employees before the rush of the evening's preparations begin.

As you would expect, our staff has become creative with this process. The dishes they make have to be quick and easy because they don't have a lot of time or energy to devote to this task. However, the daily choices are really delicious, and we thought that a few of them should appear in this book. You will enjoy preparing them when you are in a hurry or have some leftovers in your refrigerator. The Bouillabaisse is hearty and perfect for fall or winter. The Chicken Breast with the Asiago Mashed Potatoes is sure to become one of your favorites, and the Mexico-inspired Flautas won us over when we tasted this terrific meal. We're certain that you can work with any of these choices and adapt them to your personal taste. That's what our staff does every day, with fabulous results.

staff meals

the recipes

CHICKEN BREAST WITH ASPARAGUS, ASIAGO MASHED POTATOES AND MUSTARD SAUCE   154

BEEF BOURGUIGNON   157

BOUILLABAISSE   158

FLAUTAS   160

PASTA WITH VEGETABLES IN GARLIC-SHALLOT SAUCE   161

Chicken Breast with Asparagus, Asiago Mashed Potatoes and Mustard Sauce

This dish is relatively easy, and it'll look as if you spent hours preparing it. We use a European-style butter because of its higher fat content. It's better for thickening the sauce.

3 tablespoons plus 1 teaspoon unsalted butter, at room temperature, divided
1 large shallot, thinly sliced
¼ teaspoon yellow mustard seeds
1 sprig thyme
¼ teaspoon white peppercorns
1 cup white wine
Juice of ½ lemon
1 cup (2 sticks) unsalted butter, very cold, cut into pieces
4 teaspoons grainy mustard
Salt and freshly ground black pepper to taste
6 baking potatoes, peeled and coarsely chopped
1½ cups heavy whipping cream
¾ cup grated Asiago cheese
4 chicken breasts, skinned, boned, and halved
2 to 3 tablespoons oil (we like a blend of half olive and half canola)
40 spears pencil-thin asparagus, blanched in salted water, shocked in ice bath
Pinch of minced chives
Pinch of minced shallots
Fried vegetables (page 22), optional garnish

MAKES 8 SERVINGS

To make the sauce: Melt 1 teaspoon of butter in a hot skillet and toss in the shallot, mustard seed, thyme, and peppercorns. Cook for about 3 minutes. Add the wine, bring to a boil, and reduce until almost dry. Remove the pan from the heat, and add the lemon juice. Slowly whisk in the cold butter. The mixture should have a milky, creamy color. If the butter melts too quickly, it will separate. After the butter has melted, press through a fine sieve. Add the mustard and season with salt and pepper.

To make the potatoes and chicken: Boil the chopped potatoes until they are fork-tender, then drain and dry them on a sheet pan until they form a little skin on the outside. Mash the potatoes, using a fork or potato masher if you want a little more texture, a box grater if you don't. Mash the potatoes while they are still warm so they don't taste gummy. Warm the cream and 2 tablespoons of the room-temperature butter in a small pot, just until the butter melts, adding a bit of each, a little at a time, to the potatoes and stirring after each addition to make a smooth mixture. Season with salt and freshly ground black pepper. Add the cheese and stir to combine. Adjust seasonings, cover, and keep warm.

Preheat oven to 400 degrees F. Season the chicken breasts with additional salt and pepper and place in a large, ovenproof skillet with the oil blend. Sauté the chicken, smooth side down, and cook until the chicken is a caramel color, about 5 minutes. Without turning the chicken, place in the oven for about 4 minutes. Remove the chicken from the oven, let cool for 1 minute, slice on the diagonal, and keep warm.

Place the blanched asparagus in a large, hot skillet with the oil. Add the remaining tablespoon of butter, chives, and shallots, and stir until heated through, about 3 to 4 minutes. (You may need to do this in 2 batches. If so, keep the first batch of asparagus warm while you cook the second.)

To serve: Place a ring mold on each of eight large dinner plates and fill it with mashed potatoes. Remove the mold and fan 5 asparagus spears in front of the potatoes. Fan the chicken over the potatoes, spoon some sauce over the chicken and asparagus, and garnish with fried vegetables.

Wine Match: The savory, piquant mustard sauce tips the scale toward a red wine. Chicken and mashed potatoes — homey comfort food in a country setting — well, depending where your gastronomic imagination takes you, any of several wines would fit the bill. If you think American Pastoral, then a Zinfandel (*please*, red; it's the *only* kind) from California would brighten this dish with its vibrant fruit flavors. If you come from Italian ancestry, a good zippy Barbera would transport you back home. But to remain in a classical French mode, go with a Gigondas from the Rhône or a good country Fitou.

Beef Bourguignon

What an experience it is to watch the chefs at Carlos' create a lunchtime extravaganza for themselves. This is a dish that's quick and can look so special — even for a simple family meal. If you use Kobe tenderloin tips, as we do, the dish becomes a real treat. Serve it over creamy mashed potatoes.

4   pounds sirloin, cubed

Salt and freshly ground black pepper
       to taste

½   cup flour, approximately

½   cup olive oil

1   large Spanish onion, coarsely
       chopped

1   pound mushrooms (any variety),
       halved (or quartered if large)

½   cup tomato paste

1   bottle (750 ml) red wine (a
       Burgundy is our choice)

4   cups Chicken Stock (page 225), or
       Veal Stock (page 226), or beef
       broth

¾   cup coarsely chopped Italian (flat-
       leaf) parsley

8   pastry shells (optional)

Mashed potatoes (optional)

MAKES 8 SERVINGS

Liberally season the beef with salt and pepper, and coat it with a thin layer of flour. Pour the oil into a large pot over high heat. When the oil is hot, add the beef cubes and stir until they are browned. Add the onion and mushrooms, and sauté until tender, about 3 to 5 minutes. Add the tomato paste, stir, add the wine and stock, and simmer until the wine is reduced by half and the sauce has thickened, about 30 minutes. Place a portion of beef on each of eight dinner plates, sprinkle with chopped parsley, and drizzle sauce from the pot around the meat.

If you want to make this dish more elegant, first place a pastry shell in the middle of each dinner plate and half-fill it with mashed potatoes before topping with beef, sprinkling with parsley, and drizzling the sauce.

Wine Match: We don't drink at our staff meals before Carlos' opens for service, but it would be a shame if you didn't enjoy some wine with this classic dish. As the name implies, a red Burgundy would be excellent here. You may also want to try an Oregon or California Pinot Noir.

Tip: Want to add a vegetable? Serve the beef with some sautéed broccoli, spinach, or green beans. If you're using pastry shells, fan the vegetables around the shell.

Bouillabaisse

This is a traditional French fish soup. We think it's more like a fish stew because of the thick, succulent pieces of fish in the flavorful broth. This is one of our favorite lunchtime treats and is easy to make with the trimmings from various pieces of fish that we have in the kitchen. Serve it with thick, crusty French bread, add a salad, and you have a full meal.

1	tablespoon olive oil
1	small onion, diced
3	stalks celery, sliced
3	carrots, sliced into rounds
1	sprig thyme
2	quarts Fish Fumet (page 227) or clam juice

Pinch of saffron

3	small potatoes, diced
2	pounds assorted fish, cut into 1-inch cubes (we use sea bass, salmon, scallops, shrimp, octopus, mussels, and clams)
12	cherry tomatoes, halved
1	tablespoon minced chives
1	shallot, peeled and minced

Salt and freshly ground black pepper to taste

MAKES 8 TO 10 SERVINGS AS AN APPETIZER, 6 AS AN ENTRÉE

Heat a large soup pot and add the oil, onion, celery, carrots, and thyme. Cook for about 2 minutes, or until the vegetables have released some of their liquid and are translucent but not brown. Add the Fish Fumet, saffron, and potatoes, and simmer for about 10 to 12 minutes, or until the potato dice are tender.

Begin adding the fish to the broth, starting with the firmest fish (scallops first, salmon a few seconds later, then sea bass, then shrimp. Mussels and clams should be steamed open first and put on the plate before serving.) Simmer for 2 to 3 minutes until done. Add the cherry tomatoes, chives, and shallot, and season with salt and pepper. Serve hot.

Wine Match: A dish with such an abundance of seafood is versatile as far as matching it with the perfect wine. Many white wines would work well, although you should stay away from oaky choices. A Sauvignon Blanc from the Loire Valley is our choice.

Tip: If you use clams or mussels in this recipe, here's how to steam them open: Heat a pan until hot. Place the shellfish in the pan with 1 minced shallot, 1 clove of minced garlic, and salt and pepper to taste. Add about ½ cup of dry vermouth and cover the pan until the clams and mussels open. Place them in the soup just before serving. (Discard any clams or mussels that don't open.)

Flautas

Here's a quick, easy meal that's very satisfying. The name comes from the tortillas, which look like "little flutes." Many of our staff are from Mexico and bring their cooking favorites to our kitchen. This is the version most preferred by our employees, but it can easily be transformed by using shredded chicken in or on top of tortillas.

3   tomatillos, peeled but left whole

½   small onion, coarsely chopped

1   serrano chile or ½ jalapeño chile, seeds removed, coarsely chopped

1   ripe avocado, chopped

½   bunch cilantro, leaves only

Salt and freshly ground black pepper to taste

12   corn tortillas

2   cups leftover mashed potatoes

1 to 2 cups vegetable oil, as needed

6   ounces crème fraîche or sour cream (any type)

MAKES 4 SERVINGS

Prepare a sauce by placing the tomatillos, onion, and chile pepper in a small saucepot and covering with water. Simmer until the ingredients are tender, about 8 to 10 minutes. Remove ingredients from the pot and purée in a blender with about ¼ cup of the cooking water until the sauce is the desired consistency. Blend in the avocado and cilantro leaves, and season with salt and pepper.

Gently heat the tortillas, one at a time, over a flame or in a skillet, for about 5 seconds on each side (if you try to roll a cold tortilla, it may break). Place 2 to 3 tablespoons of warm mashed potatoes in a line just off-center of the surface of the tortilla, and roll into a cylinder. Hold in place with a toothpick. Repeat with remaining tortillas.

Place enough oil to completely cover the bottom of a heavy skillet, and heat the oil over medium heat. Gently sauté each rolled flauta for about 2 minutes, or until it is crisp on all surfaces, turning frequently. Repeat until all are cooked. Sprinkle lightly with additional salt and drain on a paper towel. Serve with the tomatillo sauce and a dollop of crème fraîche.

Wine Match: We can't think of anyone who would think of wine with this very traditional Mexican fare. This dish falls in beer territory. The crew at Carlos' loves Modelo Especial. Try it.

Tip: Fried foods quickly form an outer crust, so be sure to add any salt, as with this recipe, immediately after frying — before that crust forms. Ordinary table salt, not the coarser sea salt, is the condiment to use here.

Pasta with Vegetables in Garlic-Shallot Sauce

Cooking doesn't get much easier than this pasta dish. It's a favorite with our staff because it's hearty and flavorful. The lemony flavor is quite evident, so adjust the amount of juice to your own taste.

1 pound small pasta
1 small zucchini, sliced into rounds
1 small yellow squash, sliced into rounds
1 medium red bell pepper, seeded and sliced into rings
1 medium yellow bell pepper, seeded and sliced into rings
1 medium green bell pepper, seeded and sliced into rings
12 asparagus spears, tips only
1 tablespoon olive oil
Salt and freshly ground black pepper to taste
8 tablespoons (1 stick) unsalted butter, cut into pieces
3 cloves garlic, minced
1 small shallot, minced
2 teaspoons fresh lemon juice, or to taste
1 teaspoon poppy seeds
1 teaspoon minced chives
1 teaspoon minced parsley

MAKES 4 TO 6 SERVINGS

Cook the pasta in a large amount of boiling, salted water according to package directions. Drain.

While the pasta cooks, sauté, grill, or broil the zucchini and squash rounds, pepper rings, and asparagus tips with the oil. (If you're grilling or broiling the vegetables, brush them first with the olive oil. If you're sautéing them, first heat the oil in a large skillet — you may need an extra tablespoon.) Season the vegetables lightly with salt and pepper.

Meanwhile, heat the butter, garlic, and shallots over medium heat in a large skillet until the butter melts, foams, and begins to brown. Keep stirring until a nice caramel color develops. Slowly add the lemon juice and poppy seeds. Stir to combine and heat for 1 minute. Toss the sauce with the pasta, chives, and parsley. Put the pasta into a bowl and garnish with the cooked vegetables.

Note: If you'd like a heartier meal, top the pasta with grilled chicken breast or salmon filet.

Wine Match: A simple savory dish like this asks for an uncomplicated wine. The variety of vegetables tells us that we should serve a crisp white wine. If you like Pinot Grigio, here's a good dish for it. An unoaked Chardonnay also works well.

SIDE DISHES

When you go through our Entrées chapter, you'll see that each selection comes complete with "side" suggestions. Any of those options could fit in this chapter, but we decided not to separate what we saw as the essential components of each entrée. We do know how creative our home cooks can be, so we are confident you'll be able to incorporate those sides with other meals.

This chapter includes what we would consider comfort food. Try our Garlic Mashed Potatoes and you'll feel a warm, cozy sensation. Add the Dijon mustard and you'll get a bit of a zing. Gnocchi are hearty bites of pasta with exceptional flavor and texture, and you'll love the Herb Gnocchi with Mosaic Tomato Sauce that's part of this chapter. Although we haven't included wine pairings with most of these recipes, we made an exception with the gnocchi because we believe this could be a meal by itself. The Polenta is a favorite at Carlos'. It is served in many variations and works well with meat, fish, or poultry. The Mushrooms and Potatoes makes a great vegetable treat. How could we have a chapter on sides and not include a recipe for Pommes Frites? We defy you to eat just one, or even two. They are absolutely addictive!

side dishes

the recipes

HERB GNOCCHI WITH MOSAIC TOMATO SAUCE   166

ROASTED GARLIC MASHED POTATOES WITH DIJON MUSTARD   169

SOFT HERB POLENTA   170

SAUTÉED MUSHROOMS AND POTATOES   170

VEGETABLE MEDLEY   171

POMMES FRITES   171

Herb Gnocchi with
Mosaic Tomato Sauce

Gnocchi is a very hearty pasta. It can be a side dish or, with a salad and some bread, a complete meal. This version is delicious because the herbs blend into the pasta to create a bountiful bed for the light tomato sauce. When the sauce breaks, it means you've done it right; it's why we call it a "mosaic sauce." This pasta works well with other sauces as well, so try a pesto, marinara, or even just a simple sauce of butter, olive oil, and garlic.

4	baking potatoes, quartered or halved, about 3 to 4 pounds total
4	large egg whites
1	cup flour, approximately
Coarse salt and white pepper to taste	
1	large vine-ripened tomato (or ¾ cup tomato juice)
¼	cup extra-virgin olive oil
1	tablespoon unsalted butter, melted
8	tablespoons (1 stick) unsalted butter
1	teaspoon chopped fresh basil
1	teaspoon chopped fresh thyme
1	teaspoon chopped fresh sage
1	teaspoon chopped fresh tarragon
2	tablespoons chopped chives, optional garnish

MAKES 4 SERVINGS

To make the gnocchi: Preheat oven to 350 degrees F. Cook the potatoes in a steamer or in boiling water until fork-tender, about 10 to 15 minutes. Place through a ricer, then in an ovenproof pan, and place the pan in the oven for about 3 or 4 minutes, or until the potatoes are dry. Place the potatoes in a small bowl, add the egg whites, and mix by hand until well blended. Add the flour and knead the mixture until well blended. (If it appears too soft, add a bit more flour to the dough.) Season with salt and pepper.

Bring a large pot of salted water to the boil. Meanwhile, continue kneading the dough to form a ball. (Add a touch more flour if the dough is too sticky), and divide the dough into 2 or 3 balls. Roll each ball so that the dough is ½ inch thick and about 10 inches long. Cut crosswise into pieces ¾ inch long. (At Carlos' we use two forks to lightly roll each piece and to make light grooves in the dough. You can lightly pinch in the sides of each piece — or do nothing.)

Have a pot or large bowl of ice water ready on your counter. When the water is boiling, test a single gnocchi for doneness by dropping it into the water. It should float quickly, in about 1 to 2 minutes. The texture of the cooked gnocchi should be firm outside and soft inside. In small batches, place all the gnocchi in the boiling water and cook until they float. As you remove the gnocchi from the boiling water, immediately plunge them into the ice water to stop the cooking.

To make the Mosaic Tomato Sauce: Juice the tomato, season lightly with salt and pepper, and add the oil and 1 tablespoon of melted butter. The sauce will break apart, creating a "mosaic" appearance. Set aside.

In a small sauté pan over medium heat, melt the remaining butter and cook until it turns light brown (be careful not to burn it). Add the basil, thyme, sage, and tarragon, and stir to combine. Reheat the gnocchi in the melted herb butter, and stir to coat.

To serve: Place the gnocchi in a small bowl. Spoon the tomato sauce around the gnocchi, garnish with chopped chives if desired, and serve immediately.

Wine Match: Although this is usually a side dish, it can make an appealing main dish, too, and it needs less acidity and brightness in an accompanying wine because of the highly acidic tomatoes. Tomato sauces, long a quandary for sommeliers, were never a problem for the Italians when doing wine and food pairings. The Italians always knew that light reds, such as Chianti or Dolcetto, with their sturdy structure, are not bothered by tomatoes.

Roasted Garlic Mashed Potatoes
with Dijon Mustard

You'll use this recipe often. If you don't add the garlic and mustard, you'll still have great mashed potatoes. If you don't peel the skin off the potatoes, you can make the popular "smashed potatoes." For this recipe, adjust the amount of mustard that you use. Add it a little at a time until it has exactly the amount of zing that you favor. (At Carlos', we use the amount listed.)

1   whole head of garlic
½   teaspoon olive oil
4   large baking potatoes, peeled and quartered
½   cup heavy cream
2   tablespoons unsalted butter
½   teaspoon salt
¼   teaspoon white pepper
1½   tablespoons whole-grain Dijon mustard

MAKES 4 TO 6 SERVINGS

To prepare the roasted garlic: Preheat oven to 350 degrees F. Slice off the top of the garlic bulb to expose the cloves, drizzle the olive oil over the entire bulb, and wrap tightly in aluminum foil. Bake in the oven for approximately 1 hour, or until the garlic is soft but not burned. Let the garlic cool to room temperature, then gently squeeze the garlic out of each clove. Refrigerate until ready to use. Save the roasted garlic from 3 cloves for later use in this recipe.

To make the potatoes: Cook the potatoes in boiling, salted water for 20 minutes, or until they are fork-tender. Place the potatoes in the 350-degree oven for 5 minutes to remove excess moisture.

Heat the cream, butter, and the reserved 3 cloves of roasted garlic in a small pot. Cook until the butter is melted and the garlic flavor is infused in the other ingredients, about 5 minutes. Stir well to combine.

Using a food mill, rice the potatoes or mash them with a fork. Add half the cream mixture and stir to combine. Blend in the salt and pepper. Stir in the rest of the cream mixture and blend to desired consistency. Adjust seasonings. Add the mustard, stir to combine, and keep warm for serving. (If potatoes get too dry, add more cream or butter to achieve the desired consistency.)

Tip: Roasted garlic is sweet, and the unused portion from this recipe can be used as a substitute for butter on a thick, crusty baguette. It spreads beautifully and tastes great.

Soft Herb Polenta

This side dish has so many uses that the cook's only limit is his or her imagination. Polenta became widely popular in the 1990s and is now found on menus everywhere. Use it as a side dish with chicken or meat, or substitute vegetable broth for the chicken broth as a vegetarian treat.

3 cups chicken stock

Salt and freshly ground black pepper to taste

1 cup instant polenta (be sure to use instant)

8 tablespoons (1 stick) unsalted butter, cut into small pieces

¼ cup heavy cream

¼ cup grated Parmesan cheese

⅔ cup finely chopped mixed herbs (rosemary, chives, basil, chervil, tarragon, parsley, etc.) (see Note)

MAKES 4 SERVINGS

Bring the chicken stock to boil in a medium pot and season with salt and pepper. Over low heat, mix in the polenta, whisking to remove any lumps. The polenta should thicken to the consistency of loose oatmeal. Add the butter a few pieces at a time and stir until melted. Add the cream, stir to combine, and add the cheese.

Remove the polenta from the heat, fold in the herbs, and adjust seasoning. Keep the polenta warm until ready to serve. A good way to do that is to place the polenta pot in a larger pot of warm water so that the water comes halfway up the polenta pot. Stir before serving.

Note: Choose the herbs you wish, but if you are using rosemary, chop it separately because the leaves require finer chopping than the leaves of the other herbs.

Sautéed Mushrooms and Potatoes

This side dish is a welcome addition to so many entrées. Its heartiness and flavor have an earthiness that works well to warm up any meal, especially in the fall and winter.

½ cup Clarified Butter (page 220)

4 fingerling potatoes, peeled and sliced into ¼ inch rounds (see Note)

1 Portabello mushroom, sliced ¼ inch thick

8 chanterelle mushrooms, quartered

8 oyster mushrooms

8 shiitake mushrooms

Salt and freshly ground black pepper to taste

1 shallot, minced

3 chives, minced

MAKES 4 SERVINGS

Heat a medium skillet over high heat. When the skillet is very hot, add the Clarified Butter and potatoes. Sauté just until the potatoes are lightly brown. Add the mushrooms and continue to sauté. Season with salt and pepper. When the mushrooms are soft, add the shallots and stir a few minutes until the shallots are tender. Toss with the chives. Keep warm until ready to serve.

Note: Small red potatoes, or most other varieties, too, would make good substitutes.

Vegetable Medley

Use this as a side dish for almost any entrée. Our Roulade of Dover Sole (page 105) was the original home for this dish, but you'll find it welcome on most any dinner plate.

1 tablespoon unsalted butter

½ cup chanterelles, cleaned and cut into small pieces

Salt and freshly ground black pepper to taste

1 tablespoon canola or olive oil

½ cup butternut or acorn squash, cut into medium dice, blanched and cooled

½ cup brussels sprouts, washed, outside brown leaves and bottoms removed, blanched, cooled, and cut into rounds

1 medium shallot, peeled and minced

1 tablespoon minced chives

½ cup pea or daikon sprouts, cut in 1-inch lengths

½ cup radish sprouts

MAKES 4 SERVINGS

Melt the butter in a medium skillet, sauté the chanterelles in the hot butter, and season lightly with salt and pepper. Set aside. Heat a medium sauté pan, add the oil, and sauté the squash until lightly browned. Add the sautéed mushrooms and the blanched brussels sprouts. Season again with salt and pepper, and heat thoroughly. Add a bit more butter if the mixture seems dry, then add the shallots and chives and continue to heat.

When you're almost ready to serve, add the sprouts, and toss over heat. When the sprouts are warmed but still crisp, adjust seasoning. Use as directed above.

Pommes Frites

Most of the world knows pommes frites as French fries (pictured on page 165), and they are a favorite everywhere. At Carlos', we use them as a complement to our steak dishes. These are especially good sprinkled with vinegar or dipped in a spicy mustard.

4 baking potatoes, 3 to 4 pounds total

Peanut or canola oil

Salt

MAKES 4 SERVINGS

Peel the potatoes (or don't, if you'd prefer the finished fries to include skin) and use a mandoline to help cut them into small julienne slices. Soak the sliced potatoes in ice-cold water for at least 1 hour. Drain and pat dry. Deep-fry the potatoes in the oil until they are golden brown. Drain on paper towels, season lightly with salt, and serve immediately. If you don't have a deep-fryer, use 3 to 4 cups of oil heated to 350 degrees F in a heavy-bottomed, high-sided skillet.

DESSERTS

People often ask us what our all-time favorite dessert is. We can honestly say that we don't have an answer, because it seems that every time we come up with a new one, it becomes our favorite.

Many of Carlos' patrons actually plan their meals in reverse. Even before they order their dinners, they are thinking ahead to what they'll have for dessert. They always want to make sure they save room for the extraordinary treats that come out of our pastry kitchen. On any given night, they will have at least two trays of desserts to choose from. If chocolate is your passion, you will always be able to find something to soothe your craving. If you prefer fruit, you can choose something blended with a thick pastry cream, a delicate crust, or a simple bouquet of berries. It's not an easy choice. This is definitely the time of the meal when our patrons pass their plates around and share. If, somehow, there hasn't been enough sugar to satisfy your palate, a tray of beautiful Petits Fours comes out, tempting you one last time before your dinner ends.

We have chosen some of the most requested dessert recipes for this chapter. It has a diverse offering, from a dense Pave to a light Shortbread Cookie. We included a classic Crème Brûlée (easy to assemble and fun to make using a blowtorch). There is a terrific recipe for Bread Pudding and, because the world can always use another recipe for brownies, we are sharing Debbie's Brownies, with a texture and flavor beyond compare.

Although most recipes are very forgiving (with some actually encouraging experimentation), these must be followed exactly as they are written. Baking is an exact science. Although you may think you know a shortcut, don't use it. If the recipe says to sift the flour, sift the flour (sifting adds air to the ingredients and makes them lighter and fluffier; even if the flour says it's presifted, sift it). If a recipe says to refrigerate the dough, there is a good reason (usually to create a certain texture as well as to make the dough easier to work with). But one rule applies, not only to desserts, but to all our recipes: Use the freshest, highest-quality ingredients.

Unlike most other chapters of this book where we suggest a wine to pair with each recipe, choosing a dessert wine is different. Complementing the sugar content in the dessert is very much a matter of our patrons' own palates. But mostly, the number of wines suitable for dessert matches is very limited. (There's one exception. Because the Roasted Macadamia Fig Tart could be either an appetizer or a dessert, we've included a wine match for it.) We love a tawny Port with anything chocolate. Many of our patrons prefer a Sauternes, such as Muscat de Beaumes-de-Venese from France. Any of the late-harvest wines from California would be great pairings as well. We also love dessert with a crisp sparkling wine or a Chateau d'Yquem.

If you're not in the mood for something sweet, consider some French or American cheeses with delicious homemade bread, paired with one of the wines mentioned above. You could even consider making one of those wines a course in itself. Regardless of what dessert you choose, you will have a sweet, satisfying ending to your meal.

desserts
the recipes

CHOCOLATE-RASPBERRY TRUFFLES   179

BANANA-RUM BREAD PUDDING   180

SHORTBREAD COOKIES   181

PUMPKIN MOUSSE CAKE   182

OOZY CHOCOLATE CAKE   185

POACHED PEARS WITH CRÈME FRAÎCHE SORBET AND CARAMEL SPIRALS   186

STRAWBERRY-LEMON TART   189

GRAND MARNIER CHEESECAKE   190

DEBBIE'S BROWNIES   193

CHOCOLATE PAVE WITH VANILLA ICE CREAM AND ESPRESSO SAUCE   194

CHOCOLATE MOUSSE   196

HAZELNUT AND COFFEE BRITTLE   197

ROASTED MACADAMIA FIG TART   198

GÂTEAU CHOCOLAT   201

CRÈME BRÛLÉE   202

ALMOND-LEMON TART WITH MIXED FRESH BERRIES   205

Chocolate-Raspberry Truffles

Making truffles sounds difficult but it's really pretty easy and a lot of fun, and you can make them in advance. Serve them on a small tray at the end of your meal and you'll leave your guests with sweet thoughts of their special evening in your home.

13   **ounces semisweet chocolate**
½   **cup heavy cream**
1½   **tablespoons raspberry liqueur**
¼   **cup seedless raspberry jam**
½   **cup high-quality cocoa powder**

MAKES 20 TO 30 TRUFFLES

Melt 8 ounces of the chocolate over very low heat in the top portion of a double boiler, add the cream, and stir to combine. Continue cooking slowly until the chocolate and cream are incorporated and warmed through. Remove from heat and let cool. Stir in the liqueur and the jam, and place in a bowl with a cover that will seal tightly. Refrigerate for at least 2 hours, or until firm. (You can do this several days in advance.)

To make the truffles: Scoop out the chilled chocolate mixture with a small melon baller, or use a small spoon and roll the chocolate into small balls with your hands. Place the chocolate balls on a sheet pan lined with parchment paper or wax paper and return to the refrigerator for at least 1 hour, or until they have hardened.

Melt the remaining 5 ounces of chocolate in a double boiler, and roll the hardened balls in the melted chocolate just enough to coat them. Roll the chocolate-coated balls in the cocoa powder. Return the truffles to the sheet pan and refrigerate until they are set. Keep cold until ready to serve.

These little morsels are delicious and lots of fun to make. Don't be concerned if they don't look perfect the first time you try. You'll improve with practice. Until then, trust us, the taste will be superb the first time and every time.

Note: Instead of cocoa powder, you can also roll the truffles in chopped nuts of your choice. They may not look as elegant, but they will taste great.

Tip: At Carlos' we keep the truffle balls in a plastic container with ¼ cup of cocoa powder. Just before serving, we shake the container to recoat the truffles.

Banana-Rum Bread Pudding

All bread puddings are not equal. We've tried lots of them. Some are too dry, others are too soggy, but this one is just right. It's almost foolproof, it uses up all sorts of aging ingredients, and it's a real favorite in our restaurant and our home kitchen. You'll love using all those day-old breads, and don't hesitate to mix them up. We've made this dessert by mixing up cinnamon buns, brioche, and some chocolate-swirl pound cake, and you can't imagine how great that was.

4   cups cubed day-old bread (see Note)
4   ripe bananas, sliced
¼   cup dark rum
¼   cup sugar
4   large eggs
2   large egg yolks
1   tablespoon vanilla extract
½   teaspoon cinnamon (or more, to taste)
½   cup heavy whipping cream
½   cup whole milk
Vanilla or cinnamon ice cream, optional accompaniment
Caramel sauce and sliced strawberries, optional toppings

MAKES 6 SERVINGS

Preheat oven to 350 degrees F. Grease the bottom and sides of a 9 x 5-inch loaf pan.

Combine the bread cubes, banana slices, and rum in a large mixing bowl. In a separate bowl, whisk together the sugar, eggs, and egg yolks, then add the vanilla and cinnamon. In a small saucepan, combine the cream and milk, and bring to a boil. Very slowly, whisk the milk mixture into the egg mixture (not too quickly, or you'll cook the eggs), and pour over the banana-bread combination. Fold together, making sure that all the bread is well coated and soaked through.

Pour into the prepared loaf pan, and bake in the oven for 40 to 45 minutes, or until set in the middle. The top should be lightly browned. If necessary to prevent burning, cover with a foil tent and continue baking. While still warm, slice and serve. If you wish, serve with vanilla or cinnamon ice cream, or garnish with caramel sauce and top with sliced strawberries.

Note: Use any type of day-old bread. This is especially good with raisin bread, sourdough bread, or brioche.

Shortbread Cookies

These extremely rich cookies make a lovely addition to any ice cream or sorbet treat. They are also good with a layer of whipped cream and sliced fruit sandwiched between the cookies. You could also sandwich them with your favorite jam. They are supposed to be soft. But if they are too soft, add a bit of flour, subtract a bit of butter, or bake them a bit longer.

2	cups (4 sticks) unsalted butter, softened
1	tablespoon vanilla extract
1½	cups powdered sugar
3½	cups flour
½	teaspoon salt

MAKES APPROXIMATELY 3 DOZEN COOKIES (DEPENDING ON SIZE)

Beat together the butter, vanilla, and sugar in the small bowl of an electric mixer until creamy. Slowly incorporate the flour and salt at low speed. Form into dough, shape the dough into a ball, and wrap the ball with wax paper. Refrigerate until firm, about 30 minutes.

Preheat oven to 350 degrees F. Work the dough with your hands until it is pliable. Using a rolling pin, roll out the dough to about ¼ inch thick and transfer it to two flat 11 x 17-inch sheet pans, each lined with parchment paper.

Bake in the oven for 30 minutes, or until golden. Remove from oven and cut with a cookie cutter while still warm. Remove from pan when set and let cool to room temperature on a wire rack.

Tip: Watch these cookies carefully. Oven temperatures vary, and these are best removed from the oven when they are a light golden brown.

Pumpkin Mousse Cake

This cake will be a real hit for your fall dinners. Make it the day before you serve it so the mousse can set. Canned pumpkin works beautifully. If you have a gourmet shop in your area, buy some gelatin leaves. They'll last a long time in a dry place. Otherwise, buy the small boxes of gelatin at your local supermarket. Serve this cake with a scoop of vanilla ice cream dusted with some pumpkin spice or a rich caramel ice cream.

CAKE:

- 2 cups cake flour
- 1 teaspoon ground cinnamon
- 1 teaspoon baking soda
- 4 large eggs
- 1 large egg yolk
- 2½ cups sugar
- 1 can (15 ounces) pure pumpkin (approximately 1¾ cup) (see Note)
- Nonstick spray

PUMPKIN MOUSSE:

- 2½ cups heavy cream
- 1 can (15 ounces) pure pumpkin (approximately 1¾ cup) (see Note)
- 2 eggs
- 4 large egg yolks
- 6 gelatin leaves or 2 envelopes (about ¼ ounce each) gelatin
- ¾ cup sugar

ASSEMBLY AND SERVING:

- 4 ounces unsweetened chocolate, melted
- 4 ounces white chocolate, melted
- Freshly grated nutmeg
- Ice cream, optional
- Whipped cream, optional

MAKES 6 SERVINGS

For the cake: Sift together the cake flour, cinnamon, and baking soda, and set aside. In a mixer fitted with a wire whisk, beat the eggs and the yolk at low speed to combine. Add the sugar and continue beating on low speed until the mixture is light yellow and has begun to thicken, about 2 minutes or more. Add the pumpkin and stir to combine. Scrape down the sides of the bowl and mix again. Slowly add the dry ingredients, stirring as you do.

Spray the bottom of a 12 x 17-inch jelly roll pan. Place a piece of parchment paper over the sprayed bottom and press down to hold the paper in place. Spread the pumpkin batter evenly over the bottom of the pan. (At Carlos', we spread the batter on 2 jelly roll pans to create thinner layers of cake. If you do this, reduce the baking time.) Bake in a preheated 350 degrees F. oven for 12 to 15 minutes, or until the cake is golden brown. A toothpick inserted in the center should come out clean. Remove from the oven and let cool completely.

To make the pumpkin mousse: Using very cold beaters and a clean, dry, cold bowl, beat the cream until soft peaks form. Fold in the pumpkin and stir to combine. Refrigerate for 15 minutes. In the top part of a double boiler, with boiling water in the bottom, gently whisk the eggs and egg yolks. Following the instructions on the gelatin box, moisten the leaves or the contents of the envelope in a separate bowl of cold water. Add the sugar to the eggs in the double boiler, and whisk thoroughly over the boiling water. Keep whisking until the mixture warms through and the color is a light, fluffy yellow. Remove from heat and continue mixing with a hand-held beater. Add the gelatin to the egg mixture and continue to beat well until smooth and creamy. Fold in the pumpkin-cream mixture and refrigerate until set, for at least 4 hours or overnight.

To assemble in a single layer, spread the mousse over the cake and put in the freezer for at least 4 hours to harden. Remove the pan from the freezer and gently cut the cake into 3-inch squares. Place the squares on a larger, parchment-lined pan, and drizzle first with the dark chocolate, then with the white chocolate, allowing the chocolate to drip down the sides. Refrigerate.

To serve: Place 2 pumpkin squares to the side of each of six dessert plates. Dust with nutmeg. If you wish, place a small scoop of ice cream (vanilla would be good) or a dollop of whipped cream next to the cake.

Note: Be careful not to accidentally buy pumpkin-pie filling.

Note: In the photo, we have eliminated the white and dark melted chocolates and simply dusted the top with cocoa powder.

Oozy Chocolate Cake

At Carlos', we love holidays, so we always extend ourselves for special occasions like Mother's Day, Father's Day, Valentine's Day, birthdays, anniversaries, and graduations. A lot of those occasions just ooze sweetness and love, just like this dessert — which oozes chocolate, too. The warm, brownie-like texture of the cake is enhanced by the melted-chocolate center. It's like a special surprise inside. You'll love it.

10 ounces semisweet chocolate, chopped
½ pound plus 4 tablespoons (2½ sticks) unsalted butter, cut into small pieces
5 large eggs
1 cup powdered sugar
1 teaspoon vanilla extract
¼ cup very strong coffee, cooled
⅔ cup flour
2 tablespoons unsweetened cocoa powder
1¼ teaspoons baking powder
Raspberry Sauce (page 229), fruit, ice cream, whipped cream, optional toppings

MAKES 8 SERVINGS

Preheat oven to 325 degrees F. Grease eight (3-inch) bottomless ring molds or ramekins with butter or vegetable spray.

Melt the chocolate and butter over low heat in the top of a double boiler. In a separate medium bowl, whisk together the eggs, powdered sugar, vanilla, and coffee. In a separate bowl, sift the flour, cocoa powder, and baking powder, and stir to combine.

Add a small amount of the warm chocolate mixture to the egg mixture, whisking as you do. Slowly add the remaining chocolate to the eggs, whisking constantly until they are thoroughly combined. (If you add too much heated chocolate to the eggs too quickly, the eggs will cook and curdle.) Stir the flour mixture into the chocolate-egg mixture until thoroughly combined.

Pour the batter into the prepared molds or ramekins until each is about two-thirds full. At this point, you can bake, freeze, or refrigerate the batter, so long as the molds or ramekins are at room temperature when you're ready to bake. Bake in the oven for 10 to 15 minutes, or until the batter has created a dome that is slightly cracked and the sides have started to set. The setting of the sides is critical because you cannot test for doneness with a toothpick or by touching the top of the cake. Do not overbake. Allow the cakes to cool for several minutes. Serve warm in the ramekins or unmolded.

If desired, decorate around the cake by drizzling with Raspberry Sauce or with a few berries of your choice, a scoop of ice cream, or some whipped cream.

Note: If you bake these immediately, the cakes will "soufflé," meaning that they will rise very high, then fall noticeably. If you want more uniform results, let the batter rest in the refrigerator for several hours, bring to room temperature, then bake.

Note: For Valentine's Day, Carlos' serves this dessert with Crème Anglaise (page 229). Just before serving, we inject a bit of raspberry sauce into the warm chocolate center.

Poached Pears with Crème Fraîche Sorbet and Caramel Spirals

This simple dessert is a winner in the fall and winter, when pears are in season. It is light and refreshing yet sweet and satisfying — a terrific ending to any meal. If you don't have time to make the sorbet, use a creamy vanilla ice cream and make a caramel sauce instead of spirals. Or find a rich caramel sauce in the grocery store.

CRÈME FRAÎCHE SORBET:

1   **cup sugar**
1   **cup water**
2   **cups crème fraîche or sour cream**
Juice of 2 medium lemons

POACHED PEARS:

1   **cup sugar**
1   **cup water**
9   **Bosc pears (or other firm pears), 6 peeled and cored, and 3 peeled, cored, and halved**
4   **cups white wine**
1   **cinnamon stick**
1   **vanilla bean or 1 tablespoon vanilla extract**
2   **cloves**
1   **star anise, optional**

CARAMEL SPIRALS:

1   **cup sugar**
2   **tablespoons water**

FOR SERVING:

6   **mint sprigs, optional garnish**

MAKES 6 SERVINGS

To make the sorbet: Make a Simple Syrup (page 228) by combining the sugar and water in a small saucepot and bringing it to a boil, cooking until the sugar is completely dissolved. Let cool to room temperature. Pour the crème fraîche into a medium bowl, add the lemon juice, and stir in the syrup. Churn in an in ice cream maker according to the manufacturer's directions.

For the pears: Again make a Simple Syrup by combining the sugar and water in a small saucepot and bringing it to a boil, cooking until the sugar is completely dissolved. Use a small melon-baller to remove any trace of core in the pear halves. In a large pot, reduce the wine by half over medium heat, and add the cinnamon, vanilla, cloves, star anise, and Simple Syrup. Simmer for 15 minutes. Add the pears and cook approximately 20 minutes, or until the pears are fork-tender, then plunge them into cold water to stop the cooking.

To make the caramel spirals: Place the sugar and the 2 tablespoons of water in a small pot, and cook until the mixture turns a caramel color, stirring constantly to prevent burning. Allow to cool slightly. Using a spoon, drizzle the caramel in spirals around the metal handle of a whisk or other cooking utensil, turning gently to coat all sides with thin, continuous lines. Let cool briefly, then gently push off the spirals. Place the spirals on a paper towel, cool to room temperature, and store in an airtight container. These caramel spirals look fabulous and can be made in advance. One warning: if it's a humid day, prepare them just before serving or they will wilt.

To Serve: Place 1 pear half on each of six dessert plates. Place a scoop of sorbet next to the pear, and place the caramel spirals around the pear. Place a mint sprig in the sorbet for garnish.

Tip: Besides buying vanilla ice cream instead of making sorbet, you also can simplify this dish by making a caramel sauce instead of spirals. Place the sugar and the 2 tablespoons of water in a small pot and cook until the mixture turns a caramel color, stirring constantly to prevent burning. Remove from the heat and add an additional $1/4$ cup of water, stirring constantly. You'll have a sauce that can be spooned around the pears.

Strawberry-Lemon Tart

We serve this as a Valentine's Day dessert for two, but it warms the ⟨...⟩ on any occasion. Any shape mold will do. We know that you will love this easy dessert. If you are in a hu⟨...⟩ use store-bought pastry dough. You can also make this in an 8- to 10-inch tart pan with a removable bottom.

TART DOUGH:

- 2 cups flour
- ½ cup sugar
- 5 tablespoons unsalted butter, cut into small pieces
- 1 large egg
- 1 large egg yolk
- ½ teaspoon vanilla extract
- ½ teaspoon almond extract

STRAWBERRY-LEMON FILLING:

- ½ cup fresh lemon juice
- Grated zest of 1 medium lemon
- ½ cup sugar
- 6 tablespoons unsalted butter
- 3 large eggs
- 1 pint strawberries, sliced
- 5 tablespoons apricot jam

To make the tart dough: Sift together the flour and sugar, and place the mixture in the large bowl of an electric mixer. Mix on low until well blended. Add the butter, a piece or two at a time. Whisk the egg, egg yolk, and extracts in a mixing bowl, and add to the butter mixture, stirring just to incorporate. The dough should be flaky. Transfer the dough to a floured surface and knead until it feels elastic. Form a ball, cover with wax paper, and chill for at least 1 hour, or overnight.

Roll out the dough on a well-floured surface. Use a spatula to loosen and turn the dough. It should be rolled fairly thin. This is a very fragile dough, so be careful not to let it break (patch it if it does). And do not overwork the dough or it will become too sticky to shape.

Cut the dough to fit your choice of tart pan — 4 small circles or, for Valentine's Day, 2 heart shapes or a single larger tart pan. Place the mold(s) on a sheet pan lined with parchment paper and fill each shell with pie weights wrapped in parchment paper. Place the raw tart shell(s), with weights, in the freezer for 10 to 15 minutes, just to chill. (If you have dough left over, store it in the freezer.) Preheat the oven to 350 degrees F. Remove the shell(s) from the freezer and bake in the oven for 8 to 10 minutes, or just until they begin to brown. Cool the tart(s) completely before filling.

To make the filling: Combine the lemon juice, grated lemon zest, sugar, and butter in a medium pot and simmer over medium heat just until the butter is melted. Meanwhile, whisk the eggs. To create a lemon curd, temper the eggs by placing a small amount of the warm sugar mixture into the bowl with the whisked eggs, whisking constantly. Then combine eggs and the sugar mixture, again whisking constantly. Strain and cool in the refrigerator. The mixture will thicken.

Fill the cooled shell(s) with the lemon curd. Slice the strawberries and arrange them on top of the curd. Heat the jam and strain to make a glaze. (If necessary, add a bit of water to thin slightly.) Brush the glaze over the strawberries. Refrigerate the tart(s) for at least 1 hour before serving.

Although you can make the tart shell and curd a day before serving, do not assemble until the day you will be using it. Seal the shells in an airtight container. Keep the curd covered and refrigerated.

Tip: For added sweetness and a crunchier pastry bottom, melt about 1 tablespoon of white chocolate and brush a thin layer over the bottom. Allow it to harden before filling it with curd.

Grand Marnier Cheesecake

This recipe has a lot of Carlos' history behind it. When we opened the restaurant, we were up all day and half of each night creating desserts that would go well with our French cuisine. We tried tons of recipes and kept only the very best. This was one of them. It has a smooth, very creamy texture, flavored with a whisper of Grand Marnier. The chocolate-cookie crust is a bonus that is always met with enthusiastic approval. Prepare this recipe a day in advance.

CRUST:

4½ ounces (½ package) chocolate wafer cookies, ground
1 tablespoon sugar
1 tablespoon unsalted butter, melted

CHEESECAKE:

24 ounces cream cheese, room temperature
8 tablespoons (1 stick) unsalted butter, room temperature
1 cup sugar
3 large eggs, at room temperature
2 tablespoons Grand Marnier (or other orange-flavored liqueur) or more, to taste
1 teaspoon vanilla extract

GARNISH:

1 cup sugar
1 cup water
Zest of 1 orange, cut in strips, then into julienne slices

MAKES 1 (9-INCH) ROUND CAKE

Preheat the oven to 400 degrees F.

To make the crust: Combine the cookie crumbs and sugar. Stir in the melted butter and mix thoroughly to form a crust. Pat the crust into the bottom of a 9-inch springform pan. Bake in the oven for 3 minutes, or just long enough to dry the butter and melt the sugar. Remove from the oven.

Meanwhile, make the cheesecake: Blend the cream cheese, butter, and sugar in the large bowl of an electric mixer, just until smooth. Add the eggs, one at a time. Stir in the Grand Marnier, add the vanilla, and stir to combine. Pour over the baked crust and bake in the oven for 30 minutes. The cake may seem a bit runny, but that's all right. Let cool, cover, and refrigerate overnight.

For the garnish: Bring the sugar and water to a boil in a medium pot, and cover the orange strips with this Simple Syrup. Simmer and cook the zest until it is candied, about 10 minutes. Remove the strips, drain them and let them cool.

To serve: Cut the cold cheesecake into slices and top each piece with some candied orange zest.

Debbie's Brownies

This brownie recipe has been with us forever. It is not necessarily Carlos' style in terms of a fine French pastry, but it sure makes a fine dessert. The batter is very thick (thicker than you might expect), producing an incredible, fudgy taste sensation. We sometimes add a cup of dark chocolate chips — it makes an even denser brownie with an added chocolate chunk.

1²⁄₃ cups sugar

8 tablespoons (1 stick) unsalted butter, softened

4 ounces unsweetened chocolate, melted

2 large eggs

1 tablespoon water

1½ teaspoons vanilla extract

1⅓ cups unbleached flour

¼ teaspoon baking soda

1 cup chocolate chips, more or less to taste, optional

Confectioners' sugar, optional

MAKES ABOUT 18 BROWNIES

Preheat oven to 350 degrees F. Grease a 9 x 13-inch pan.

Combine the sugar, butter, melted chocolate, eggs, water, and vanilla extract in a large mixing bowl, add the flour and baking soda, and stir well to combine. The batter will be very thick. If you want to add chocolate chips, fold them in here. Pour and scrape the batter into the greased pan and bake in the oven for 25 minutes, or until a toothpick inserted in the center comes out clean. Do not overbake. Let cool completely, dust with confectioners' sugar, if desired, and cut into squares.

Tip: For easy cutting, place pan of brownies in the freezer for approximately 1 hour. Cut with a very sharp-edged knife.

Chocolate Pave with Vanilla Ice Cream and Espresso Sauce

The name *pave* comes from a French reference to the bricks used to pave the streets. It refers to both the shape of the slices and to the dense texture. You must make this dessert in advance. The day before works well. Although this recipe tells you how to make the ice cream, buy a high-quality, rich, vanilla-bean ice cream if you'd prefer. This dessert has an incredible chocolate flavor, and small slices provide a big sensation.

PAVE:

10	ounces bittersweet chocolate
4	tablespoons (½ stick) unsalted butter
4	large eggs, separated
⅛	teaspoon cream of tartar
2	tablespoons sugar

ICE CREAM:

4	cups milk
3	vanilla beans
1	cup sugar
14	large egg yolks

ESPRESSO SAUCE:

3	cups milk
1	teaspoon ground espresso or coffee extract
6	large egg yolks
½	cup sugar

MAKES 4 TO 6 SERVINGS

To make the pave: Melt the chocolate and butter in the top part of a double boiler. Remove from heat and let cool. In an electric mixer, beat the egg whites and cream of tartar until foamy. Add the sugar and continue beating until the mixture is stiff. Add the egg yolks to the cooled chocolate. Fold one-quarter of the whites into the chocolate mixture, then add the remaining whites and fold until completely incorporated. Pour into a 7-inch rectangular mold that has been placed on a cookie sheet lined with wax paper. Smooth to even the surfaces. Refrigerate for at least 6 hours or overnight. Just before serving, unmold the pave.

To make the ice cream: Heat the milk with the vanilla beans in a large pot. Whisk together the sugar and the yolks in a large mixing bowl and slowly add the hot milk. Return the mixture to the pot, place over medium heat, and stir constantly with a wooden spoon until the mixture is thick enough to coat the spoon. Strain into a bowl over an ice bath, let cool, and mix in an ice cream maker according to the manufacturer's directions.

To make the espresso sauce: Heat the milk with the espresso or extract in a medium pot. Whisk the yolks and sugar in a small bowl, then slowly add a small amount of the hot milk mixture, whisking constantly. Add the remaining milk mixture, return to the heat and stir constantly with a wooden spoon until the sauce coats the spoon. Strain into a bowl over an ice bath.

To serve: Cut the pave into ½-inch slices and place 2 slices on individual plates. Surround with the espresso sauce, and place a small scoop of ice cream to the side.

Tip: To unmold the pave, place a warm towel around the edges of the mold for a few moments and invert onto a tray. If you prefer, you could make this in individual molds.

Tip: Instead of making espresso sauce, you could dust the pave with cocoa powder and surround it with fresh seasonal berries.

Chocolate Mousse

Making chocolate mousse is relatively easy. It is one of our all-time favorites and seems to find its way into almost all of our dessert offerings. You can make this same recipe substituting white chocolate and, if you make both, you can serve a portion of each in a parfait glass and create beautiful layers. This recipe also works great in a trifle bowl, layered with chocolate chips or other favorite toppings. Be creative and come up with your own fabulous dessert.

2¼ cups sugar, divided
1 cup water
1 pound bittersweet chocolate
8 large egg whites
1 quart heavy cream
Additional heavy cream, whipped for
    topping, optional
Mint leaves, for garnish
6 to 8 plain cookies, for garnish

MAKES 6 TO 8 SERVINGS

Combine 2 cups of the sugar and the water in a medium pot, bring to a boil, and cook until the mixture reads 234 degrees F on a candy thermometer (at which point the mixture will form a soft ball). From time to time, brush the insides of the pan with water to prevent crystals from forming. Remove the pot from the stove and let the mixture cool for 2 minutes.

Melt the chocolate in the top portion of a double boiler. Keep the melted chocolate warm but not hot.

Whip the egg whites in an electric mixer fitted with a wire whip until soft peaks form. Slowly add the remaining ¼ cup of sugar. Let the egg whites cool for about 2 minutes, then slowly add the hot sugar-water mixture in a very fine stream. Make sure the bowl isn't getting too hot. Slowly fold in the chocolate mixture by hand, being careful not to overmix.

In a separate bowl, whip the heavy cream until soft peaks form and fold into the chocolate mixture. Spoon into individual small bowls or ramekins and refrigerate until firm. Serve with a dollop of fresh whipped cream and garnish each plate with a fresh mint leaf and a cookie.

Tip: We use three garnishes at Carlos' — whipped cream, mint leaves, and cookies — but for everyday serving at home, you can dispense with any of them.

Hazelnut and Coffee Brittle

This recipe creates "nougatine" to use as a sprinkle over ice cream — or to just eat plain. It is delicious inside baked apples, pears, or plums. It will melt slightly, but that only enhances the flavor. Instead of hazelnuts, you could use macadamia nuts, walnuts, or other favorite nuts. Use your culinary creativity and you'll probably come up with many clever uses for this crunchy treat. This recipe may be made 1 week in advance and kept in an airtight container at room temperature.

1½ cups sugar
⅔ cup light corn syrup
½ cup water
Juice of ½ medium lemon
1½ cups chopped hazelnuts
¼ teaspoon salt, optional
½ teaspoon baking soda
½ cup coarsely chopped espresso coffee beans
½ teaspoon vanilla extract

MAKES 6 TO 8 SERVINGS

Combine the sugar, corn syrup, water, and lemon juice in a medium pot and bring to a simmer over medium heat. *Do not stir.* Using a damp pastry brush, wash down the insides of the pot with water as crystals begin to form, but be careful not to touch the liquid. Cook for approximately 10 to 15 minutes, or until the temperature on a candy thermometer reads 150 degrees F. Add the nuts, stir to combine, and cook until the temperature of the mixture reads 315 degrees F. Add salt, baking soda, and coffee, stir to combine, add the vanilla, and stir again. Remove from heat.

Pour the mixture (which will be hot and sticky) onto a silicone mat or a jelly roll pan that has been sprayed with vegetable oil. Tip the pan on an angle so the mixture spreads. Use a pot holder to hold the pan as it will get very hot. *Be careful not to touch the hot brittle, which could cause a severe burn.* Let cool completely. Chop the brittle into small pieces, and store in an airtight container.

Roasted Macadamia Fig Tart

We love this dessert because of the combination of the salt from the nuts and the sweetness of the fruit. It would be delicious served with vanilla ice cream. Although it is not often the case, this dish could also be served as an appetizer, and many of our patrons love to use it as a brunch dish. Because it's so versatile, we have included a wine note for this tart.

ROSEMARY-FIG CURD:

¾ cup water
1 to 2 sprigs rosemary
3 large egg yolks
1 cup sugar
8 tablespoons (1 stick) unsalted butter, in small pieces
½ cup chopped figs (fresh or dry)

FILLING:

1 to 1½ pounds macadamia nuts, finely chopped
Salt to taste, if necessary
1 cup light brown sugar, tightly packed
¾ cup light corn syrup
1 teaspoon vanilla extract
2 tablespoons unsalted butter, in small pieces
3 large eggs, beaten
1 (8 to 10-inch) sweet tart shell, pre-rolled and unbaked, store-bought or from a standard recipe

MAKES 1 (10-INCH) TART

To make the fig curd: Bring the water and rosemary to a boil. Meanwhile, combine the egg yolks and sugar in a small mixing bowl. When the rosemary-water mixture is boiling, add a small amount to the yolk mixture, stirring as you do, then slowly whisk in the rest. Place that mixture, the butter, and the figs into a medium saucepan over medium heat, and stir the curd as it comes to a simmer. Strain and chill.

To make the nuts and filling: Preheat oven to 350 degrees F. Place the nuts on a sheet pan. If they are not already salted, season with salt and roast for about 6 to 10 minutes, until golden. Meanwhile, place the brown sugar, corn syrup, vanilla, and butter in a medium saucepan, and bring to a boil, stirring constantly to prevent the sugar from burning on the bottom. Beat the eggs in a large mixing bowl. Pour a small amount of the hot sugar mixture into the eggs, stirring as you do, then slowly whisk the remaining mixture into the eggs. Let cool to room temperature and refrigerate for 5 to 10 minutes.

To assemble: Spread the curd gently onto the tart shell, sprinkle the nuts on top of the curd, stir, and pour the chilled filling almost to the rim of the shell. Bake in the oven, still at 350 degrees F, until set, about 25 minutes. Chill for clean slicing. Serve warm.

Note: If you'd like to use the tart dough recipe on page 189, substitute the almond extract with vanilla extract.

Wine Match: This is a very sweet dish. If you choose to serve this tart as a dessert, find a good port wine or an Oloroso sherry — either combines well with the sweet, nutty flavors. If you approach it as an appetizer, look for a still wine, such as a full-throttle Zinfandel.

Tip: Roasting and salting the macadamia nuts enhance their flavor.

Gâteau Chocolat

Although the basic translation of this French title is "Chocolate Cake," this dessert is much more than that. Rich, creamy, sinfully dense with a blend of different chocolate textures, this cake would make any occasion a reason to celebrate.

CHOCOLATE GENOISE:

1   **cup sugar**
10   **large eggs**
¾   **cup flour**
¼   **cup cocoa powder**
Unsalted butter and flour, for cake pan

MOUSSE, GLAZE, AND GARNISH:

20   **ounces semisweet chocolate, divided**
⅓   **cup heavy cream, scalded**
5   **cups heavy whipping cream, divided**
Simple Syrup (page 228)
Fresh berries, optional garnish

To make the chocolate genoise: Whip the sugar and eggs for 10 minutes on high speed in an electric mixer until stiff. Preheat the oven to 350 degrees F. Combine the flour and cocoa powder, and fold in the egg mixture, a third at a time. Butter and lightly flour a 10-inch-round cake pan. Pour the batter into the pan and smooth the top. Bake in the oven for 15 minutes, or until set and a toothpick comes out clean. Cool in the pan for about 20 minutes, or until the cake begins to shrink from the sides. Invert and unmold the cake and let it cool completely.

Make chocolate mousse by melting 8 ounces of the chocolate in the top part of a double boiler. Heat the scalded heavy cream just until it starts to bubble, then whisk it into the melted chocolate. Let cool slightly. Whip 2 cups of the heavy whipping cream until soft peaks begin to form and fold it into the cooled chocolate mixture.

Make a glaze by melting the remaining 12 ounces of chocolate in the top of a double boiler. Meanwhile, heat the remaining 3 cups of heavy whipping cream just until it begins to bubble. Slowly add the hot cream to the melted chocolate about a third at a time, and mix to combine.

To assemble and serve: Cut off the rounded top of cake with a serrated knife, and slice the rest of the cake in half horizontally. Flip over the top half so that the bottom becomes the top. Lightly brush with the Simple Syrup, and spread a layer of the mousse over the syrup. Place the two cake layers together so the mousse and syrup are in the middle. Brush what is now the top with a thin layer of Simple Syrup and top with a layer of mousse. Smooth with a spatula. Refrigerate for 1½ hours. When set, glaze the cold cake on a cooling rack with a pan underneath, lined with wax paper. Pour the glaze over the cake and let it drip down to coat the top and side of the cake. Refrigerate again to set.

To serve: Just before serving, cut into slices with a warm knife. Surround with fresh berries, if desired.

Tip: Simple Syrup, such as you'll make for this recipe, is an ingredient you'll use in many desserts and some sauces. It is aptly named because making it is extremely simple. It's a condensed, liquid form of sweetener. It works best when it is cold, so for best results, make it the day before you'll use it and refrigerate it overnight. It will keep in the refrigerator in an airtight container for a few weeks.

Crème Brûlée

This traditional French dessert rates high on everyone's list. The best brûlée has a very creamy texture that's not too heavy. The top should form a thin, crunchy layer that melts in your mouth, creating a perfect balance of flavor and texture. Because you can make this in advance, it's the perfect ending to a fabulous dinner party, and your guests will be very impressed with your ability to use a blowtorch.

3   cups heavy whipping cream
1½ cups milk
1¼ cups sugar
1   vanilla bean, slit open and seeds scraped out and reserved
2   large eggs
7   large egg yolks
Coarsely granulated sugar
Fresh berries

MAKES 6 TO 10 SERVINGS

Pour the cream and milk into a medium saucepan and, over medium heat, scald the mixture. Stir in the sugar, the scrapings from the vanilla bean, and the bean itself. Once the sugar is dissolved, remove from heat.

In a separate bowl, whisk the whole eggs and the yolks just enough to break up the yolks. Place a small amount of the warm milk mixture into the bowl with the eggs, stir, then slowly add the remaining milk mixture, stirring constantly. Strain to remove any remaining milk solids and the vanilla bean. Set aside.

Preheat oven to 275 degrees F. Fill small ramekins almost to the top with the mixture and place the ramekins in a pan with sides high enough so that water that will reach halfway up the sides of ramekins. Bake on the bottom rack of the oven for 1½ hours, or just until set. Watch to avoid overcooking; you do not want the crème brûlée to brown in the oven. Cool for 30 minutes, refrigerate to chill thoroughly, and, when cooled, cover with plastic wrap. You can make them up to 2 days in advance.

Before serving, sprinkle with coarsely granulated sugar. Using a blowtorch, lightly brown the tops. Serve on a dessert plate surrounded with fresh berries.

Tip: You can buy a small blowtorch at your local hardware store or gourmet shop. You'll find some very small ones for sale, and they work really well. Use this handy appliance to brown meringues, too, such as for pies and Baked Alaska.

Almond-Lemon Tart with Mixed Fresh Berries

The shortbread crust on this tart uses powdered sugar instead of granulated for a softer dough texture. The crust provides a sweet, crunchy bottom for the refreshing almond-lemon filling. We use blueberries and raspberries at the restaurant for a perfect combination of tart and sweet flavors. But it would be delicious, too, with tiny melon balls.

CRUST:

2	cups all-purpose flour
½	cup powdered sugar
1	teaspoon almond extract
½	teaspoon salt
1	cup (2 sticks) unsalted butter, chilled and cut into ½-inch pieces

FILLING:

1	cup sliced almonds, toasted and finely chopped (to resemble bread crumbs)
½	cup almond paste (about 5 ounces)
½	cup sugar
4	teaspoons grated lemon peel
2	large eggs
⅓	cup whipping cream
½	cup fresh lemon juice

FOR SERVING:

3½	pints raspberries
1	pint blueberries
	Whipped cream
	Raspberry Sauce (page 229), optional garnish

MAKES 8 SERVINGS

Preheat oven to 425 degrees F.

Place the flour, sugar, almond extract, and salt in food a processor fitted with a steel blade, and pulse to combine. Add the butter pieces a few at a time and continue pulsing until moist clumps form. Gather the dough together in a ball and knead until the dough is smooth.

Press the dough into an 11-inch tart pan with a removable bottom. Top with a sheet of parchment or wax paper and fill with pie weights, beans, or uncooked rice. Place the crust in the freezer for about 20 minutes, or until firm, to relax the gluten, prevent shrinkage, and help prevent the dough from puffing up during baking.

Remove the crust from the freezer and bake until the sides set and begin to turn brown, about 15 minutes. Remove the paper and weights, and bake the crust until cooked through and pale golden in color, about 10 to 15 minutes. Pierce the crust with a fork to crush any bubbles and bake for 10 minutes longer. Let crust cool completely.

Before making the filling, reduce the oven setting to 350 degrees F.

In a food processor fitted with a steel blade, blend the chopped almonds, almond paste, sugar, and lemon peel. Add the eggs, cream, and lemon juice, and process until blended. The mixture will be very loose. Pour into the cooled tart crust. The mixture should come almost to the top of the pan.

Bake the tart in the preheated oven for about 40 minutes, or until the top feels firm to the touch and the edges are golden. Let cool completely, cover, and refrigerate. The tart can be prepared to this point up to a day in advance.

To serve: Let stand at room temperature for 30 minutes. Carefully push up the bottom of the tart pan to release the tart, and place the tart on a platter. Cut into wedges, place on individual plates, and top with berries and whipped cream. If desired, surround with Raspberry Sauce.

Tip: For a crunchier crust, melt white chocolate and brush the bottom and the sides of the tart shell. Let it harden and then fill.

DRESSINGS AND OILS

So many of our customers want to know the secret behind our delicious dressings and oils. The secret is that we use the freshest ingredients and make new dressings and oils frequently. There are some fine bottled products, but there is no comparison to the just-blended flavors of our oils and dressings.

Take a minute or two to read this section and you'll see that making these staples takes only a few minutes. The dressings are especially easy. What really makes the difference is the quality of the oils, vinegars, and herbs that you choose to use. If you are using olive oil, make sure that it is the highest grade. Use an extra-virgin olive oil for dressings and drizzles, but don't ever heat it. The flavor is best in a cool state.

When choosing a balsamic vinegar, don't listen to people who say that the age makes no difference. Sample a two-year-old balsamic and a twenty-year-old balsamic and you'll know instantly which is better. The rich flavor and dense texture of the aged balsamic make a world of difference. Is it expensive? Yes, but you need to use much less of the expensive vinegar because it is so reduced and intense. Must you spend a lot of money on special ingredients? Yes and no. No, you could certainly produce a good flavor with the less-expensive versions, but the highest grades yield an exceptional flavor.

We use fresh herbs for our dressings. Although dried herbs are okay, the freshest herbs will bring on a flavor burst and a dimension that cannot be obtained with the dried variety. We use only kosher or coarse salt because we think it better enhances the overall flavor.

When you make oils that require vegetables — such as red peppers, beets, and tomatoes — follow the directions and you will produce oils that will enhance many dishes. You are certainly not limited to the ones in this book. Store your oils in tightly covered containers and they will last for at least three weeks in the refrigerator. They are great for both their flavor and their decorative qualities. Be sure to shake them lightly before using.

dressings & oils

the recipes

BALSAMIC VINAIGRETTE 210

BASIL VINAIGRETTE 210

CHOPPED SHALLOT BALSAMIC VINAIGRETTE 211

GINGER VINAIGRETTE 211

ASIAN VINAIGRETTE 212

ROASTED RED PEPPER AND DILL DRESSING 212

BASIL OIL 213

BEET-HAZELNUT OIL 213

SWEET PEPPER OIL 214

ROSEMARY OIL 214

TOMATO OIL 214

Balsamic Vinaigrette

Use this simple recipe as a salad dressing, as a coating for oven-dried tomatoes, or in whatever way your imagination suggests. You'll find lots of great uses for this recipe.

½ cup balsamic vinegar
Pinch of coarse salt
Pinch of white pepper
1½ cups canola or olive oil

MAKES ABOUT 2 CUPS

Season the vinegar with salt and pepper. Slowly add the oil and whisk until well blended. Adjust seasoning to taste. Use as directed. Store covered in the refrigerator.

Tip: Although some recipes using balsamic vinegar require an expensive, aged balsamic, this isn't one of them. To give this dressing a specific taste that you like, add some chopped fresh herbs, such as oregano, thyme, or basil.

Basil Vinaigrette

We make this vinaigrette by using the residue of basil leaves that have been strained from making Basil Oil (page 213). It is delicious served over a salad of tomatoes and mozzarella cheese, or over any other lettuce-based salad. A favorite at Carlos' uses this recipe over mixed greens with toasted pine nuts and slivers of Blue d'Auvergue (or any blue cheese or light Gorgonzola).

3 tablespoons basil residue from Basil Oil (page 213), or more to taste
2 tablespoons champagne vinegar
½ cup olive oil and/or canola oil
Salt and freshly ground black pepper to taste

MAKES ABOUT ½ CUP

Combine the basil residue and vinegar in a medium bowl. Slowly add the oil, whisking as you do, until well blended. Season with salt and pepper. Use as directed. Store covered in the refrigerator.

Chopped Shallot Balsamic Vinaigrette

This dressing reflects the punch of the shallots. You can, of course, adjust that punch to your personal taste. Try this dressing on a leafy green salad, or make a bruschetta by spreading it on toasted baguette rounds. We're sure you'll find many creative uses for this pungent vinaigrette.

¼ cup balsamic vinegar
1 cup extra-virgin olive oil
2 teaspoons chopped shallots
Salt and freshly ground black pepper
    to taste

MAKES 4 SERVINGS

Combine all the ingredients with a wire whip. Blend well before using. Store covered in the refrigerator.

Ginger Vinaigrette

This dressing is delightful on a salad of Bibb lettuce, thinly sliced daikon (or common red radishes), and finely chopped chives. Use it to make an hors d'oeuvre by placing a small piece of seared tuna or poached shrimp over some shredded greens, drizzling with this dressing, and topping with a sprinkle of chopped chives.

½ cup pickled ginger, with liquid
1 cup seasoned rice wine vinegar
½ cup canola oil
½ cup crème fraîche or sour cream
1 teaspoon salt
⅛ teaspoon black pepper

MAKES 6 SERVINGS

Process the ginger in a blender until finely chopped. Blend in the vinegar and canola oil. Strain through a fine sieve, return the liquid to the blender, and add the crème fraîche. Blend, add the salt and pepper, blend again, and adjust seasoning to taste. Store covered in the refrigerator. Whisk well before using.

Asian Vinaigrette

This dressing is great on a salad with lettuce, mandarin oranges, cashew nuts, and crunchy Asian or rice noodles. It can also be used with seared tuna placed over brown rice and garnished with slivered vegetables, or use it to marinate chicken breasts.

¼   **cup soy sauce**
¼   **cup sesame oil**
2 tablespoons sherry vinegar
2 tablespoons rice wine vinegar
½   **cup water**
¼   **cup sugar**

MAKES ABOUT 1½ CUPS

Whisk together all the ingredients. If you are not using immediately, refrigerate the dressing and whisk again just before serving. Store covered in the refrigerator.

Roasted Red Pepper and Dill Dressing

This dressing must be prepared in advance — and it's well worth the effort. The taste of roasted pepper is unique and it gives this dressing a full-bodied flavor.

2   **roasted red peppers, halved and seeded**
1   **tablespoon olive oil**
1   **medium onion, chopped**
2   **cloves garlic, minced**
¼   **cup heavy cream**
1½ **teaspoons chopped fresh dill**
Salt and freshly ground black pepper to taste

MAKES ABOUT 1½ CUPS

Preheat oven to 350 degrees F. In a gas oven, broil the peppers on a foil-lined jelly roll pan just until their skins begin to blacken; in an electric oven, place the peppers a few inches from the heating element. Turn the peppers so that the skin will blacken all around. When finished, place the peppers in a brown paper bag for 30 minutes and their skins will slip off easily.

Meanwhile, heat the oil in a small skillet and sauté the onion just until translucent. Add the garlic and continue to sauté, being careful not to let the garlic brown. Place the skinned roasted peppers, onion-garlic mixture, cream, and dill into a blender and purée. Strain through a fine sieve into a small pot and heat through, but be careful not to let it boil or the dressing will separate. Season with salt and pepper, and refrigerate at least 4 hours before serving over mixed greens, or use as directed. Store covered in the refrigerator.

Tip: Roasted peppers have many culinary uses. If you roast the peppers, skin them, cover them with flavored oils, and let them sit overnight to absorb the oil, you'll have a great appetizer. Another option is to take a piece of flatbread or sliced and toasted baguette, smear it with blue cheese, and top with roasted peppers, or use them atop other vegetables. Just use your imagination and you'll come up with many more ways to use roasted peppers — and this dressing.

Basil Oil

This oil, one of Carlos' most popular, keeps for up to two weeks in the refrigerator. The same basic mix can be made with cilantro, arugula, parsley, or chervil.

2 cups basil leaves, stems removed
1 cup canola oil
Salt and freshly ground white pepper to taste

MAKES ABOUT 1 CUP

Steam the basil leaves for about 4 minutes, just until wilted. Place the hot basil leaves in a blender (they infuse better when they're hot), add the oil, salt, and pepper, and blend on high for a few minutes until the mixture is very thick. Pour into a glass container and refrigerate overnight to create a strong flavor. Remove from the refrigerator, strain through a fine sieve, and return to the refrigerator until ready to use. The residue can be used in another recipe, Basil Vinaigrette (page 210). Use as directed.

Tip: At Carlos' we use this oil so much that we store it in a plastic squeeze bottle for quick and easy access.

Beet-Hazelnut Oil

This oil nicely complements many recipes — particularly those made with duck— because of its woodsy taste. It is also terrific for some of your favorite chicken recipes, as a salad dressing, or drizzled over asparagus. Be sure to prepare this at least 5 hours in advance so all the flavors can infuse the oil.

1 shallot, coarsely chopped
1 clove garlic, smashed
1 cup balsamic vinegar
1 cup fresh beet juice (from 2 to 3 large beets)
¼ cup vegetable oil
¼ cup hazelnut oil
2 tablespoons olive oil
1 teaspoon sesame oil
1 teaspoon soy sauce
1 teaspoon sugar
1 teaspoon salt
½ teaspoon white pepper
1 teaspoon balsamic vinegar, if needed

MAKES ABOUT 2 CUPS

In a small saucepan, combine the shallot, garlic, and vinegar, and, over medium-low heat, reduce to a thin syrup. Add the beet juice and reduce again to a thin syrup. (Watch carefully to prevent burning.) Skim off any foam as you reduce, then let cool to room temperature. Strain the cooled reduction through a fine strainer into a medium bowl.

Slowly whisk in the oils, soy sauce, sugar, salt, and pepper. Continue whisking gently until the ingredients are well blended. Add the balsamic vinegar if you'd like a more pronounced vinegar taste and/or to thin the oil. Adjust seasonings. Whisk vigorously before spooning onto plates as directed in other recipes. Serve at room temperature, but store covered in the refrigerator. This oil may be made up to 2 weeks in advance.

Sweet Pepper Oil
This oil is wonderful with a fresh herb salad or other vegetable dishes of your choice.

2   red bell peppers, seeds and stem removed

2   yellow bell peppers, seeds and stem removed

1/4   cup canola or olive oil

Salt and freshly ground black pepper to taste

MAKES ABOUT 1 CUP

Process the peppers separately in a juicer. Combine 1/2 cup of red pepper juice and 1/2 cup of yellow pepper juice, and reduce to a syrup consistency by cooking in a small saucepan over medium heat for 15 to 20 minutes, stirring occasionally to prevent burning. Slowly whisk the oil into the hot syrup and season with salt and pepper. Chill. Use as directed. This oil can stay refrigerated for up to 2 weeks.

Rosemary Oil
This oil is perfect with fish or on salad.

2   cups canola oil

5 to 6 large sprigs rosemary

Salt and freshly ground black pepper to taste

1   teaspoon black peppercorns

1   bay leaf

MAKES ABOUT 2 CUPS

Place all the ingredients in a medium pot and heat over low heat for 30 minutes. Strain and reserve oil. Use as directed in other recipes. This oil can be kept for up to 2 weeks in the refrigerator.

Tomato Oil
This delicious oil complements any salad. It should be made in advance to allow the flavor to infuse into the oil.

2   large tomatoes, skin on and quartered

2 to 3 sprigs thyme

1   large clove garlic, whole

1/4   cup tomato paste

3   cups canola oil

Salt and freshly ground black pepper to taste

MAKES ABOUT 3 CUPS

Place all ingredients in a medium saucepot and cook over low heat for 2 to 3 hours. While it's still hot, strain through a fine-meshed strainer. Use as directed. Store in the refrigerator for up to 2 weeks.

BASICS

This chapter contains recipes that we use many times with many different foods in the course of a day. Most of them are easy to prepare and we think that you will enjoy using them with our suggested recipes — or by coming up with new ways to complement some of your own culinary creations.

Some are just basic cooking items, such as the recipe for Clarified Butter. Our recipe for Brioche is terrific. There is almost nothing better than the aroma of bread baking in your oven. Our recipe for Oven-Dried Tomatoes is quite simple and can be used in dressings, on crostini, tossed in salads, or as a garnish to another vegetable. The Roasted Garlic Purée is great in mashed potatoes or simply as a spread for a thick, crusty piece of French bread. The Raspberry Sauce and Crème Anglaise are standards for many of our desserts.

basics

the recipes

CLARIFIED BUTTER   220

BEURRE BLANC   220

BEURRE ROUGE   221

GARLIC HERB BUTTER   221

ONION RELISH   222

ROASTED GARLIC PURÉE   222

OVEN-DRIED TOMATOES   223

TOMATO COULIS   223

ROASTED VEGETABLE STOCK   224

CHICKEN STOCK   225

LAMB STOCK   225

VEAL STOCK   226

LOBSTER STOCK   226

FISH FUMET   227

RED WINE SYRUP   227

BRIOCHE   228

SIMPLE SYRUP   228

CRÈME ANGLAISE   229

RASPBERRY SAUCE   229

Clarified Butter

Many recipes call for clarified butter. Clarified butter (also called drawn butter) is unsalted butter that has been melted and heated so that the water has evaporated and the milk solids have separated. Those particles will fall to the bottom. When they're removed, you'll be left with pure butterfat. Clarified butter allows for higher temperatures when sautéeing since those milky parts have already been removed. Make it in larger batches, if you wish; it will keep, covered, for about 2 weeks in the refrigerator, 6 months in the freezer.

1   cup (2 sticks) unsalted butter

MAKES ABOUT 3/4 CUP

Melt the butter in a pan over low heat. It will separate. Skim off the foamy white portion, which is milk fat, and discard. Continue to heat the butter slowly until it turns clear. Some milk fats may cling to the bottom, so ladle off the clear (clarified) butter into a metal container with an airtight lid. Use as directed.

Beurre Blanc

This is one of the most basic sauces in cooking. It welcomes the addition of numerous flavorings so it can be tailored for hundreds of dishes.

1   cup (2 sticks) unsalted butter, cut into pieces and divided
1   shallot, diced
6   peppercorns
1   bay leaf
½   bottle (750 ml) dry white wine
Juice of ½ small lemon
Salt and freshly ground black pepper to taste

MAKES ABOUT 1 CUP

Melt a teaspoon or so of the butter in a shallow pan over medium heat. Place the shallot, peppercorns, and bay leaf in the pan, and sweat the vegetables for about 1 minute, being careful to prevent them from browning. Add the wine and reduce until only about ¼ cup of the liquid remains, about 10 minutes, and it is a deep straw color. Add the lemon juice and remove from heat for 1 minute.

Add the remaining butter, a piece at a time, whisking until each piece is melted before adding the next. It's best to move the pan on and off the heat; you want enough heat to melt the butter but not so much that the mixture burns. The important thing is to whisk continually until the sauce is smooth. Strain the sauce into a small container, season with salt and pepper, and keep the sauce warm by placing the container in a pot of warm (not hot) water. Use as directed.

Beurre Rouge

Carlos' version of this sauce really wakes up its flavor. The ingredient you would least expect is espresso. The sugar gives it a nice boost, too. Try Beurre Rouge on salmon or scallops. This recipe's cousin, Beurre Blanc, is on page 220.

1 cup (2 sticks) unsalted butter, cut into pieces and divided
1 shallot, diced
6 peppercorns
1 bay leaf
½ bottle (750 ml) dry red wine
1 tablespoon espresso
1 tablespoon sugar
Juice of ½ small lemon
Salt and freshly ground black pepper to taste

MAKES ABOUT 1 ½ CUPS

Melt a teaspoon or so of the butter in a shallow pan over medium heat. Place the shallot, peppercorns, and bay leaf in the pan, and sweat the vegetables for about 1 minute, being careful to prevent them from browning. Add the wine, espresso, and sugar, and reduce until only about ¼ cup of the liquid remains, about 10 minutes, and the mixture is a deep red. Add the lemon juice and remove from heat for 1 minute.

Add the butter, a piece at a time, whisking until each piece is melted before adding the next. It's best to move the pan on and off the heat; you want enough heat to melt the butter but not so much that the mixture burns. The important thing is to whisk continually until the sauce is smooth. Strain the sauce into a small container, season with salt and pepper, and keep the sauce warm by placing the container in a pot of warm (not hot) water. Use as directed.

Garlic Herb Butter

Sometimes it seems like this flavored butter goes in almost every recipe. Our chefs reach for it often. Check the freshness date on your butter; that's how long it will keep. We store it in a plastic, airtight container, but you could slice off and freeze pieces in freezer bags, and then thaw the pieces as you need them. Add chopped fresh herbs, such as basil or tarragon, and you'll love how much this can contribute to your chicken, vegetable, fish, and meat dishes.

1 cup (2 sticks) unsalted butter, softened
¼ cup parsley, leaves only, chopped
3 cloves garlic, minced
1 tablespoon Pernod

MAKES ABOUT 1 CUP

Place all the ingredients in the workbowl of a food processor, fitted with a steel blade. Pulse until the ingredients are combined well.

Tip: Do not use the garlic that you can buy in supermarkets already peeled. It has no flavor. We understand how this became a convenience product, but there is no comparison to a dish made with fresh garlic. The flavor is so much more intense. This is not the place to take a shortcut.

Onion Relish

This relish is a delicious addition to a dinner with fish, oysters, or beef. Prepare the relish a day in advance to let the flavors blend. If you don't like mushrooms, omit the Portabello. It adds a nice texture and flavor but is not essential to enjoy this meal-enhancer.

1   cup red wine vinegar
½   cup water
2   cloves garlic, minced
1   medium red onion, peeled and finely chopped
2   teaspoons salt
¼   teaspoon white pepper
5   tablespoons sugar
1   teaspoon finely chopped thyme leaves
¼   cup olive oil
2   yellow bell peppers, coarsely chopped
2   red bell peppers, coarsely chopped
1   large Portabello mushroom

MAKES 4 SERVINGS

Combine the vinegar, water, garlic, and onion in a medium mixing bowl. Add the salt, pepper, and sugar, and mix again. Add the thyme, oil, and chopped peppers. Mix thoroughly, and set aside. Scrape off the top layer of the mushroom and gently remove the ribs underneath. The mushroom should basically be white, but it's fine if a little brown remains. Marinate the mushroom in the onion relish for at least 1 hour, or overnight in the refrigerator.

Remove the mushroom from the marinade and grill. Slice the grilled mushroom, add the slices to the onion relish, and stir to combine.

Roasted Garlic Purée

Have you ever noticed garlic's charming incongruity? Uncooked, it is bitter and pungent, but cooked it becomes softer and more fragrant. This recipe is evidence that the smooth texture and abundant flavor of roasted garlic will provide many uses. You will love it puréed in mashed potatoes. Just squeeze out the cloves and you'll have a delicious spread for some crusty French bread, or mix it with some fresh vegetables.

1   large head garlic, papery skins left on
2   tablespoons olive oil
½   cup water, approximately

MAKES ½ TO ¾ CUP

Preheat oven to 350 degrees F. Using a sharp knife, cut off the top of the garlic head to expose the ends of the garlic cloves (see photo on page 217). Brush the entire head with the olive oil and place it in a small, shallow pan filled with about 1 inch of water. Bake for 45 to 60 minutes, or until garlic is soft and golden brown. Squeeze out the contents of each clove, and purée in a blender or food processor. Use as directed in various recipes in this book.

Oven-Dried Tomatoes

Make as many tomatoes as you like. This recipe is so flexible that we've dispensed with a yield and most quantities. Once the tomatoes have been dried in the oven, they keep for a week in an airtight container in the refrigerator. Slice them and toss them in your pasta with some broccoli, pine nuts, roasted garlic, and your favorite sauce. Chop them and mix with fresh basil, garlic, and a touch of Balsamic Vinaigrette and you'll have a great topping for bread or to serve over grilled fish.

Large tomatoes (or plum tomatoes), cored, seeded, and quartered
Balsamic Vinaigrette (page 210, or store-bought)
Salt and freshly ground black pepper to taste
1   very thin slice garlic per tomato wedge
Thyme leaves

Place the tomatoes on a rack that has been placed on a foil-lined sheet pan with sides. Brush with a light coat of Balsamic Vinaigrette and lightly sprinkle the tomatoes with salt and pepper. Place 1 thin slice of garlic on each tomato piece and lightly sprinkle each piece with thyme leaves.

Bake at your lowest possible oven setting for 4 to 6 hours, or until shriveled. The tomatoes will not be totally dried out. There will still be some moisture content.

Tomato Coulis

This coulis is perfect over fish, on the side of grilled chicken, or tossed with pasta. We are sure you will find many uses for this easy sauce.

1   tablespoon olive oil
2   fennel bulbs, coarsely chopped
20 plum tomatoes, peeled and seeded
2   cups Chicken Stock (page 225)
2   tablespoons toasted fennel seeds

MAKES 3 TO 4 CUPS

Heat the olive oil in a large pot, add the chopped fennel, and cook over medium heat until translucent. Add the tomatoes, Chicken Stock, and fennel seeds. Cook the tomatoes over medium-low heat, stirring occasionally, until the sauce has thickened, about 35 to 45 minutes. Purée the sauce in batches in a blender, covered with a damp dishtowel. Strain through a medium sieve. Serve warm.

Roasted Vegetable Stock

This is a terrific stock that can be used in many recipes. Many people use it as a substitute for chicken broth. We think it works especially well with our risotto. Keep this stock in the refrigerator for a few days or in the freezer for up to six months.

ROASTED VEGETABLES:

1	tablespoon vegetable oil
2	garlic cloves, crushed
1	large shallot, chopped
2	carrots, cut in medium dice
1	large Portabello mushroom, cut in medium dice
¼	fennel bulb, cut in medium dice (or 1 teaspoon fennel seeds)
2	medium leeks, white parts only, cut in medium dice
3	parsnips, cut in medium dice
2	plum tomatoes, cut in medium dice
1	small onion, cut in medium dice

BROTH:

½	cup dry vermouth
⅔	teaspoon black peppercorns
½	teaspoon chopped fresh rosemary
½	teaspoon fresh sage
½	teaspoon dried oregano
1	bay leaf
4	quarts cold water

MAKES ABOUT 4 QUARTS

Preheat oven to 400 degrees F. Combine the vegetable oil and garlic with all the vegetables. Place the vegetables on a pan and roast them in the oven for 1 hour, stirring once or twice.

Place the vermouth, peppercorns, rosemary, sage, oregano, bay leaf, and cold water in a stockpot, add the roasted vegetables, and simmer for 45 minutes. Strain and cool. Refrigerate for a few days or freeze for up to 6 months. There will not be any fat to skim from the top.

Chicken Stock

This recipe is a basic for many recipes at Carlos'. It is used in our soups, sauces, and risotto. It is simple to prepare, but it does take time to make a really good, clear stock. It is important to cook the stock slowly over low heat. It will keep in the refrigerator for up to three days, but it can stay in the freezer for 6 months.

5	pounds chicken bones, wing tips, gizzards
5	quarts cold water
2	large onions, coarsely chopped
2	large carrots, cut into 1-inch pieces
3	ribs celery, cut into 1-inch pieces
6	parsley stems
1	sprig thyme
1	bay leaf
1	teaspoon peppercorns

MAKES ABOUT 4 QUARTS

Place the chicken bones and parts and the water in an 8-quart stockpot, and heat to a simmer. Skim the foam off the top of the water. Add the onions, carrots, and celery, and simmer for 2 hours, skimming occasionally. Add the parsley, thyme, bay leaf, and peppercorns, and simmer for 2 to 3 hours more. Strain, let stock come to room temperature, and refrigerate for up to 3 days or freeze for up to 6 months. Thaw if frozen, use as directed in recipes in this or other cookbooks, or use in place of water for cooking rice. Before using, skim any congealed fat from the surface.

Lamb Stock

This is an incredibly flavorful stock. Note that we haven't mentioned or listed salt in this recipe or any other of our stock recipes. That's because the flavors of a stock change with each hour of simmering and reducing, and many of them present a very strong flavor of their own without the need for salt. When the stock is refrigerated or frozen, the ingredients can change again. Also, these stocks are used in recipes that themselves use salt, so we avoid giving the stock a salty presence of its own.

6 to 8	pounds lamb bones
2	tablespoons vegetable oil
2	medium onions, coarsely chopped
3	ribs celery, cut in 1-inch pieces
2	carrots, peeled and cut in 1-inch pieces
½	cup tomato paste
1	cup dry red wine
5	quarts cold water
6	parsley stems
1	sprig thyme
1	bay leaf
1	teaspoon peppercorns

MAKES ABOUT 4 QUARTS

Preheat oven to 400 degrees F. Place the lamb bones on a jelly roll pan and roast them for 30 to 45 minutes. While the bones are roasting, heat the oil in a large stockpot and sauté the onions, celery, and carrots for about 10 minutes, or until they are thoroughly browned. Add the tomato paste and cook for 2 minutes. Deglaze the pot by adding the red wine and cook until the volume has been reduced by half. Add the roasted lamb bones, scraping any bits at the bottom of the roasting pan into the stockpot. Add the water, bring to a simmer, and add the parsley, thyme, bay leaf, and peppercorns.

Simmer for 2 hours, skimming occasionally. Strain, cool, and use as directed in recipes in this book. You can refrigerate this stock for about 3 days or freeze it for 6 months. Before use, skim off any fat that has congealed on the top.

Veal Stock

This stock takes about 8 hours to cook — but most of that is untended time. It's important to steadily simmer the stock without letting it boil. From time to time, skim off any impurities that rise to the surface. As with all stocks, start with very cold water to help draw out the juices and the best flavors.

6 to 8 pounds veal bones
2 tablespoons vegetable oil
2 medium onions, coarsely chopped
3 ribs celery, cut into 1-inch pieces
2 carrots, cut into 1-inch pieces
½ cup tomato paste
1 cup dry red wine
5 quarts cold water
6 parsley stems
1 sprig thyme
1 bay leaf
1 teaspoon peppercorns

MAKES ABOUT 4 QUARTS

Preheat oven to 400 degrees F. Roast the veal bones in the oven for 1 hour.

Heat a large stockpot, heat the oil in the pot, and sauté the onions, celery, and carrots until they are thoroughly browned, about 10 minutes. Add the tomato paste and cook for 2 minutes. Deglaze the pot by adding the wine and cooking until the volume has reduced by half. Add the veal bones, scraping any bits from the bottom of the roasting pan into the stockpot.

Add the water and simmer for about 6 hours. Add the parsley, thyme, bay leaf, and peppercorns. Skim occasionally and simmer for 2 more hours. Strain the stock and let it cool to room temperature. Use as directed, skimming any fat from the surface before you do. Refrigerate for up to 3 days in an airtight container or freeze for up to 6 months.

Lobster Stock

For this stock, you need use only the shells of the lobster, so cook the meat separately and use it to make a delicious lobster salad or a pasta dish. You needn't clean out the body cavity, but you do need to remove the claws and the tail. Be sure to let the stock come to room temperature before refrigerating or freezing it.

1 tablespoon unsalted butter
1 large onion, cut in small dice
2 large carrots, cut in small dice
3 ribs celery, cut in small dice
5 mushrooms, quartered
3 to 4 pounds uncooked lobster shells (claws and tails removed)
2 teaspoons tomato paste
¼ cup brandy
¼ cup dry white wine
4 quarts cold Fish Fumet (page 227) or cold water
6 parsley stems
1 bay leaf
1 sprig thyme
12 black peppercorns

MAKES ABOUT 4 QUARTS

Melt the butter in a stockpot and "sweat" the onion, carrots, celery, and mushrooms in the butter, cooking for about 3 to 4 minutes. Add the lobster shells and cover the pot until the shells are bright red, approximately 5 to 7 minutes. Add the tomato paste, stir, add the brandy, and cook until the liquid has almost evaporated. Add the wine and cook until it has almost evaporated. Add the Fish Fumet or water, stir to combine, and add the parsley, bay leaf, thyme, and peppercorns.

Simmer for 45 minutes. Strain, leaving any sediment on the bottom of the pot. Use as directed in other recipes. After letting the stock cool to room temperature, it can be refrigerated for about 3 days or frozen for up to 6 months. Before using, remove any congealed fat from the surface (there shouldn't be much).